A FIRST BOOK OF THE LENS.

*AN ELEMENTARY TREATISE
ON THE ACTION AND USE OF THE
PHOTOGRAPHIC LENS.*

BY

C. WELBORNE PIPER.

LONDON :

HAZELL, WATSON, AND VINEY, LIMITED,

1, CREED LANE, LUDGATE HILL, E.C.

1901.

PRINTED BY
HAZELL, WATSON, AND VINEY, LD.,
LONDON AND AYLESBURY.

CONTENTS.

Contents.

A FIRST BOOK OF THE LENS.

CHAPTER I.

LIGHT AND OPTICS.

1. LIGHT AND OPTICS.—The science of optics is derived from the study of the natural composition and
propagation of light; visible light being a manifestation
of certain forms of energy. A knowledge of optics
enables us, with the aid of certain appliances, to so control
the composition and transmission of light as to produce
certain desired effects.

In photography we employ a lens to produce inside a
camera an image of such objects as come within a certain
outside range of view; and the purpose of this book is
to explain the manner in which such an image is produced,
and the rules governing its production under varying
conditions. Our main subject of study is, therefore, the
photographic lens, but its action cannot be well understood or explained without a preliminary knowledge of
the theories of light and optics.

All that we know of light is derived from the study of
its effects, and by a logical process, supplemented as far
as possible by experimental tests, a theory with regard
to the constitution and propagation of light has been
evolved, upon which is based the science of optics. This
theory of light is of such a nature that we can look at

it from two points of view, and evolve from it two optical theories, perfectly compatible with one another in all respects, and dependent on each other; one is known as physical optics, and the other as geometrical optics. Both lead to the same result; but while the geometrical theory is in most cases more easily understood and applied, an appeal to the physical theory will usually more quickly elucidate a knotty point. As the result of the existence of two optical theories, there are always two methods of expressing an optical fact, and one mode of expression being sometimes more convenient than the other, it is advisable to have at least a distinct appreciation of the difference between the two theories.

2. THE THEORY OF LIGHT.—Under the accepted wave theory, light is nothing but a travelling undulation in an imperceptible hypothetical medium called ether, which is supposed to pervade all space throughout the universe. Such a travelling undulation may be illustrated by dropping a stone into a pond of still water, and observing the circular series of ripples that apparently move outward from the point of impact in all directions. This apparent outward movement is an illusion: it is not the water but the undulation only that travels. All the movement that really takes place is a circular over-and-over motion in a vertical plane of each particle of water in succession; as the particles rise they form ripples, as they fall troughs are produced between the ripples. But, though the water does not move outwards, an impulse is imparted from one particle of water to the next which eventually causes the undulations to extend over the whole surface of the pond. This impulse may be considered to travel in straight lines radiating outwards in all directions from the centre of the ripples, while the circular ripple that at any particular period is farthest from the centre denotes the limit to which the impulse has at that moment reached. The primary cause of the ripples is of course the impact of the stone upon the water, and the point of impact is the starting point of the impulse which causes the ripples.

Applying this analogy to the case of light, we may look upon a source of light as the source of an impulse, or energy, that imparts an undulatory wave or ripple-like

motion to the particles of ether.* These wave movements
do not, however, take place on a plane surface, but in
the interior of a mass; and therefore the movement which
denotes the limits to which the impulse at any particular
moment has reached, does not take the form of a circular
ripple on a plane surface, but forms the surface of a
sphere, the centre of which is the source of energy, and
the radius of which is equal to the distance travelled by
the impulse. As the light travels farther and farther
into space there is produced a continually advancing and
expanding spherical wavefront due to the continually progressing impulse, which travels at a certain velocity in
straight lines direct from the source of light.

In optics we are concerned mainly with the effect of
placing obstructions of various kinds in the way of the
travelling energy and wavefront. A lens is nothing but
a temporary obstruction placed in the way of the light,
and the effect of such an obstruction is that the direction
of the impulse is changed, and the form of the wavefront
altered, just as the circular form of the water ripple is
altered if it meets an obstruction in the pond. This is
the point where the two theories of optics start. We
may study only the effect of the obstruction on the wavefront, which is physical optics; or we may confine ourselves
to the study of the effect of the obstruction on the direction
of the impulse, which is geometrical optics. In either
case we shall arrive at the same result, for under all
conditions the direction of impulse is normal to the wavefront, and so the two change together.

3. PHYSICAL OPTICS.—Assume that we have a source
of light in the shape of a point as at P (figs. 1 and 2),
and that at L we have a lens. Under the physical theory,
from P there is a progressive expanding series of concentric wavefronts, a, a, a, etc., the advance of which
(disregarding all light that does not actually meet the
lens) is temporarily hindered by the lens, which, though
transparent, is of denser substance than the air. The
thickness of the lens being variable, the obstruction offered

---

* These ether ripples are not exactly comparable with the water
ripples, and the analogy must not be pushed too far.

by it also varies; hence the curvature of the wavefront
is altered. If the greatest obstruction is offered by the
centre of the lens, as in fig. 1, the convex wavefront is
flattened during its passage through the glass and becomes
concave as it leaves it, as shown at *b, b, b*, etc., and when
free of the lens it contracts as it progresses towards the
point *Q*, on which point the altered directions of impulse
now converge. This point is a focus. If there is no

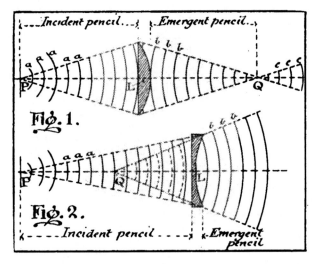

further obstruction in the way after having contracted
to a focus the continued impulse causes the wavefront to
again expand. The focus is then practically a new source
of light, and the new expanding wavefront is convex as
shown at *c, c, c*, etc.

If the greatest obstruction to the passage of the light
is offered by the margins of the lens, as in fig. 2, the centre
of the wavefront progresses more rapidly than the margins,
and the whole becomes more convex, and, when free from
the lens, expands more rapidly, and as if it originated from
a point *Q* between the lens and the original source of
light *P*. The point *Q* is then a focus, differing from *Q*

in fig. 1 in that it is an unreal or "virtual" focus instead
of a real one. In fig. 1 the light really contracts on
to *Q*, but in fig. 2 it only appears to expand from the
focus. This virtual focus is also in effect a new source
of light. Fig. 1 illustrates the effect of the type of lens
known as positive, fig. 2 that of the one known as a
negative lens.

4. GEOMETRICAL OPTICS.—We will now consider the
action of a similar pair of lenses from the point of view
of geometrical optics. In figs. 3 and 4 again let *P*
represent the source of light, but, instead of showing the

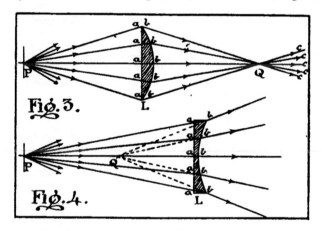

expanding wavefronts, let the lines *Pa* represent a few
of the directions of impulse of the energy emanating from
P; as before ignoring all light that does not actually
meet the lens. Altering the nomenclature to suit the
accepted conventions of geometrical optics, we call these
lines of direction of impulse or energy "light rays."

All rays that are obstructed by the lens, excepting only
the one that is exactly normal to the lens surface, are bent
at the points of contact *a*, *a*, etc., and after passing through
the substance of the lens they are again bent at the second
surface at the points *b*, *b*, etc., again excepting the one
ray that meets that surface normally. After the second

bending they are either actually convergent on (as in fig. 3) or apparently divergent from (fig. 4) the focus Q. After intersecting each other at the focus Q in fig. 3, the rays again diverge, in the absence of an obstruction, as shown at c, c, c, etc.

This is a very convenient but conventional theory; light rays do not actually exist while wavefronts are a real conception. To explain why the conventional light rays are bent at the surfaces of the lens we must look upon them as normals to wavefronts, and resort to the true physical theory; but, in most cases, we can more easily trace and explain the action of lenses with the aid of the geometrical theory. It must, in future, be understood that reference to light rays implies that we are looking at whatever matter is under consideration from the geometrical point of view, while mention of wavefronts implies that we are taking up a physical standpoint.

It is easy to remember the distinction between the two theories if we clearly understand that :

(*a*) In physical optics we consider only the form of the travelling wavefront.

(*b*) In geometrical optics we consider only the direction of movement of particular points in the travelling wavefront.

(*c*) Any point in a wavefront moves in a direction normal to the wavefront.

5. SPHERICAL ABERRATION.—If from any cause a focus, such as that shown in figs. 1 to 4, is either not formed perfectly, or is misplaced, aberration is considered to exist. If in either of the illustrated cases the altered wavefront is not perfectly spherical, the various altered directions of impulse, which are always normal to the curved surface, cannot either converge upon or diverge from one point, and a true or sharp focus cannot be formed. This particular aberration, due to non-sphericity of the wavefront, is known as spherical aberration. A lens so designed and constructed as to ensure perfect sphericity of the altered wavefront, is called aplanatic, while if spherical aberration exists the lens is non-aplanatic.*

* Special attention should be given to these definitions, as various

6. COLOUR.—We cannot thoroughly understand the theory of light without studying that of colour, for colour is an effect of light, which indicates by its variations the existence of varieties of light.

Going back to our simile of the ripples on the pond, it is evident that the size of the ripples depends on the size of the stone, and the force with which it strikes the water, for a small pebble will raise only small ripples while a large rock will produce big waves. Also, a succession of stones thrown into the water will produce a succession of systems of ripples. Something similar to this takes place at a source of light. The ether undulations vary in size with the force of the impulse that starts them, and the primary causes of the impulse being various, and continually at work, innumerable series of undulations of different sizes are continuously travelling from the source. Ordinary daylight, as we appreciate it, is composed of a number of undulations varying in size—both as regards wavelength, or the length of an undulation measured from crest to crest of each ripple, and as regards amplitude, or height measured from the top of the crest to the bottom of the trough. The effect produced by the undulations depends on their wavelength and amplitude, colour varying with the former and intensity with the latter.

A wavefront of white light is therefore not formed by a simple undulation, but by a number of undulations, and when it meets the surface of a medium such as glass the resistance offered varies with undulations of different wavelength. Glass offering the greatest resistance to the passage of undulations of the shortest wavelength the different sets of undulations become separated, each forming its own wavefront; those which meet with the greatest resistance forming wavefronts of the greatest curvature, or shortest radius.

writers attach various meanings to the terms "spherical aberration" and "aplanatic." This note applies also in the case of other definitions of technical terms. No two authors seem to agree throughout in matters of nomenclature, and students are often confused by the various applications of the same word. The knowledge that such differences of expression exist, should, however, be an efficient safeguard against any misapprehension.

7. CHROMATIC ABERRATION.—Suppose P (fig. 5) to be a source of compound light emitting two series of undulations of different wavelength or colour, say red and violet. The colour of the light will then be a compound of red and violet. Let a, a, a represent the expanding wavefront of compound light progressing from P to the lens L. During the passage through the lens the violet light, which is composed of undulations of very short wavelength, is more retarded than the red, and it therefore forms a wavefront of its own (as indicated by the dotted curves b, b, b), which, being of greater curvature than that of the red light (indicated at c, o, c), contracts to a focus at a nearer point, at Q_1 instead of Q. Thus there are two foci formed, one of violet and one of red light.

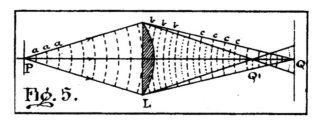

Fig. 5.

If we draw rays normal to the different wavefronts, as shown by straight lines on the diagram, we find that what we may call a single compound ray from P splits up at the point of contact with the lens into two rays, one of which we may call the violet ray, and the other the red, each of which goes to its own focal point. To understand this it is necessary to remember the conventional nature of a ray of light.

This chromatic aberration can be corrected by combining different materials in one lens to so control the direction of the separated rays of various colours that they may re-combine at the focal point, and so produce a focus of the same colour as the original light. A lens so adjusted is styled achromatic for such colours as are thus recombined, while it is non-achromatic, or possesses chromatic aberration, in the case of any colours which come to different foci. If the light is very complex the lens is generally achromatic for certain colours only, and non-achromatic for the rest. If achromatic for more than two colours it is sometimes styled apochromatic.

It should be understood that in considering light and colour we deal only with a comparatively small number of ether waves. The longest visible ethereal wave is only about twice the length of the shortest, and light and colour only covers an octave or so in a mighty scale of graduated ethereal waves of unknown limits. Some of the invisible waves beyond the visible light octave are of importance to the photographer. The visible vibrations give the colour effects of red, orange, yellow, green, blue, and violet, with intermediate shades; and, in addition to such colour effects, these same vibrations give effects of heat and chemical action, the former being most intense at the red end of the scale, and the latter at the violet end. Beyond the visible red we have infra-red vibrations which produce more powerful heat effects, and beyond the visible violet we have ultra-violet vibrations of great chemical or actinic energy, and it is by this ultra-violet invisible "light" that the photographic image is mainly produced. In an achromatic photographic lens the visible vibrations by which we focus, and the actinic vibrations by which the image is produced must come to the same focus, but in a lens that is to be used solely for visual purposes, the latter vibrations need not be considered, and the lens need only be achromatic for the brighter visible light; hence a lens may be perfectly achromatised for use in a lantern, but non-achromatic for use in a camera. Thus, there are varying degrees of achromatism.

8. LIGHT PENCILS.—Referring again to figs. 1 to 5, it is easily seen that only a small portion of the total amount of light emanating from the source P is actually transmitted by the lens. No light outside the dotted lines in figs. 1 and 2, and the corresponding rays in figs. 3 and 4, is utilised. The limited quantity of light that falls on the lens forms a pencil of light incident to the lens, and this pencil has the form of a cone with a convex spherical base or wavefront. On the opposite side of the lens we have an emergent pencil also forming a cone, the

apex of which is the focus. The incident and emergent
pencils together form a double pencil of light, which in
the case of a positive lens consists of two cones base to
base. The incident pencil is divergent, while the emergent
pencil is convergent. The diameter of the pencil is (in the
diagrams) limited by the diameter of the lens; and, the
lens being circular, a transverse section of the pencil is
also circular, if the source of light is directly in front of
the lens, but elliptical if the pencil passes obliquely through
the lens.

If the source of light is removed to an extreme distance
from the lens, the length of the incident pencil becomes so
much greater than its diameter that the rays composing
it become practically parallel, and its wavefront practically
plane. In such a case it is sufficient to consider the pencil
to be truly parallel with a plane wavefront, or to be
cylindrical instead of conical in form.

When light passes through a series of lenses, a pencil
emergent from the first lens is incident to the second, and
so on. Such intermediate pencils may have either concave,
convex, or plane wavefronts—*i.e.* they may be convergent,
divergent, or parallel. If the series of lenses is used as a
photographic combination, the incident pencil to the first
lens must be either parallel or divergent, while the emergent
pencil from the last lens must be convergent.

9. APERTURE.—In the preceding diagrams the greatest
diameter of the incident pencil is limited by the diameter
of the lens, but, actually, it is limited either by the brass
mounting of the lens, or by a metal diaphragm or stop placed
near the lens. However limited, the greatest diameter
of the incident pencil is the diameter of the " effective "
aperture of the lens. It is important to remember
that the effective aperture of a lens does not necessarily
correspond with the actual aperture of the diaphragm, and,
also, that it is liable, under certain conditions, to vary in
diameter with variations in the distance of the object.
This is especially the case when a diaphragm is placed a
little distance from the lens. The effective aperture for
a parallel pencil is then less than it is for a divergent
pencil from a near object, and the nearer the object the
greater becomes the aperture, until its expansion is limited

by some other mechanical obstruction. This inconstancy of aperture is one of the small matters that are commonly neglected by photographers.

The aperture for a parallel pencil is always taken as the standard or nominal aperture of the lens, and variations are universally ignored, with the result that some apparently sound theoretical principles in connection with the use of lenses break down to a certain extent in practice. The matter of aperture will be frequently alluded to again. The term nominal aperture is frequently applied to the actual diaphragm aperture to distinguish it from the effective aperture. The term is not, however, used in that sense in this book.

10. REFRACTION.—So long as a pencil of light is travelling in one medium only, its wavefront remains unaltered and its rays continue to travel in straight lines. When, however, it meets the surface of a second medium of either greater or less density, or resisting power, the form of the wavefront is altered, while the rays are bent or deviated from their original course, as has been shown in figs. 1 to 4. This deviation, or alteration in form of wavefront, is called refraction, and a surface at which it takes place is a refractive surface. The degree to which a refracted ray of a certain wavelength is deviated from its original course, depends, first upon the angle at which the incident ray meets the surface, and second upon the relative density, or resisting power, or relative refractive power of the two media; every two media capable of transmitting light having a certain constant refractive power for light of a certain wavelength or colour.

Relative refractive power is represented by the ratio of the relative velocities of light in the two media, and this ratio is styled the relative refractive index. The velocity of light of any colour is constant in a vacuum, and different media are classified according to the refractive indices from a vacuum. The ratios are then styled absolute refractive indices, but they do not differ greatly from the relative refractive indices from air into the several media.

The greater the refractive index of any medium, the

greater the deviation produced in a ray entering that
medium. Thus the absolute refractive indices of flint
and crown glass being respectively 1·57 and 1·52, any
particular ray falling on a surface of flint glass suffers
greater deviation than a similar ray meeting a surface of
crown glass at the same angle.

The angle of incidence of a ray on a refractive surface
is measured, not from the surface, but from a normal to
the surface. In fig. 6 two surfaces (*abc*) are shown, one
curved and the other plane, the description applying to
either indiscriminately. The surface may be considered
to be one separating air and glass. Consider *db* to be
a ray of light of a certain fixed colour, or wavelength,
passing through air and striking the surface of the denser

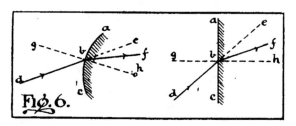

Fig. 6.

medium in the point *b*. Instead of continuing straight
on to *e*, it suffers deviation from its original course to
the extent of the angle *ebf*, which is the angle of deviation.
Through *b* draw *gh* normal to the surface—that is, at
right angles to the plane surface, and radial to the curved
surface, the centre of which is at *h*. The direction of the
light being from *d* to *b*, the ray *db* is incident to the
surface *abc*, its degree of incidence being measured by
the angle *dbg*, which is known as the angle of incidence.
The angle *fbh*, made by the refracted portion of the ray
with the normal *bh*, is the angle of refraction, and the
sine of this angle is equal to the sine of the angle of
incidence divided by the relative refractive index from
air into glass; or, to put the relationship of the angles
in another form, the ratio of the sine of the angle of
incidence to the sine of the angle of refraction equals

the relative refractive index. This is called the law of sines.

The course of a ray of light is always reversible, and we may assume that in fig. 6 the light travels from f to b in the glass and is then refracted to d. The angle of incidence is then the angle fbh, and the angle of refraction is gbd, while the deviation is the same as before: that is, it is equal to ebf. The ratio of the sines of the angles of incidence and refraction is now the converse of the former ratio—*i.e.* if, when the light passes from air into glass the ratio (or the relative refractive index) equals μ, then when the light passes from glass into air the ratio or index is $1/\mu$. Supposing light to pass through two refractive surfaces, such as those of a lens, it first passes from air into glass and then from glass into air, so that the ratio of the sines at one surface is the reciprocal of that at the other.

If the surfaces are parallel the angle of incidence at the second surface is equal to the angle of refraction at the first, and the angle of refraction at the second surface is equal to the angle of incidence at the first, therefore the first incident and last emergent rays are parallel. The surfaces may be considered to be parallel when their normals are parallel, and this condition may be fulfilled with any form of lens as well as with plane surfaces.

When a ray, after undergoing refraction and deviation at the several surfaces of a lens, finally emerges in a direction parallel to its original course we may consider that the lens has produced refraction without deviation, or that the ray is displaced but not deviated from its original direction. Sometimes, however, with a certain arrangement of lenses the ray may ultimately be free even from displacement, and pursue a course in continuation of its original one. When a pencil of light falls upon a lens, one ray (if the whole surface of the lens is utilised) must pass free from deviation, and that ray is called an axial ray, but it is not necessarily the central (or "chief") ray of the pencil.

In fig. 6 there are some points to be noticed in connection with the deviation of rays.

(a) When a ray passes from a light medium into a dense one it is refracted towards the normal—*i.e.* bf is nearer bh than is be.

2

(*b*) When a ray passes from a dense medium into a light one it is refracted away from the normal—*i.e. db* is farther from *gb* than would be a continuation of *fb*.

(*c*) The angle of deviation is equal to the difference between the angles of incidence and refraction,—*i.e. ebf = dbg — fbh.*

(*d*) The greater the angle of incidence the greater are the angles of deviation and refraction.

11. DISPERSION.—As the refractive power of a particular medium varies with rays of different colours or wave lengths, compound rays are separated at the point of incidence on that medium. Let a ray *db* (fig. 7) of combined red and violet light fall on a glass surface *abc* at *b*, and, as before, let *gbh* be normal to that surface. As the violet

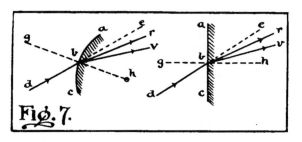

Fig. 7.

light suffers greater deviation than the red, the former takes the direction *bv*, while the latter takes that of *br*. The degree to which the rays are separated depends on the difference between the refractive powers of the glass for red and violet rays. This separation is known as dispersion, and the degree of dispersion is represented by the angle *rbv* which equals the difference between the deviations of the two rays. The dispersive power of a medium for two rays of particular colours thus varies with its refractive indices for those two colours. The dispersive power of any one medium varies with different pairs of rays, and, to express it, it is necessary to specify the particular colours and to take some one particular colour as a standard of reference.

12. REFLECTION.—When light falls on a surface at an angle with the normal, part only of the light suffers

refraction ; a certain quantity is reflected in an opposite
direction. Thus in fig. 8 a ray *db*, incident on the
surface *abc*, of either a dense or rare medium is partly
refracted in the direction of *bf*, or *bk*, and partly reflected
in the direction *bm*, the angle of reflection *gbm* being
(under the law of reflection) equal to the angle of incidence
dbg, both angles being measured from the normal *gh*.
There is therefore a certain loss of intensity in the refracted ray, and if there are a number of refractive
surfaces in succession, there may be considerable total
diminution of light owing to the loss at each surface.

The greater the angle of incidence, the greater is that
of reflection, and the greater is the amount of light
reflected and lost. To obviate excessive loss of intensity

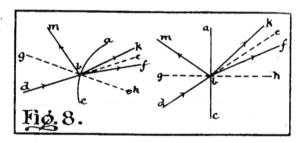

Fig. 8.

of light, it is advisable to avoid an excessive number of
reflecting surfaces, and also to avoid very oblique angles of
incidence. Oblique light must be employed, but by careful
selection of curvatures for the refracting surfaces very
oblique incidence may be to a certain extent obviated.

When a refracting surface is a separating surface
between two different kinds of glass, reflection may be
diminished by cementing the two surfaces together with
some medium, the refractive index of which is approximately the same as the glass. This renders the lens more
nearly homogeneous in structure : that is to say, it brings
the two different glasses into optical contact without any
separating film of air, and, as the less the difference in
density of the media bounding a refractive surface the
less is the loss of light by reflection, surfaces between

glass and glass are of less consequence than those between glass and air.

If we assume the surface *abc* to be that of a rare medium, and the angle of incidence to be so great that the still greater angle of refraction would come to 90°, refraction does not take place, and the whole of the light is reflected. This is known as total reflection, and the angle of incidence at which total reflection takes place is called the "critical" angle of the dense medium. Reflection and refraction together combine to produce false images, in addition to the true one due to refraction only, and these false images are the cause of the effect known as Flare.

CHAPTER II.

13. LENSES.—A lens may be defined as an isolated portion of a medium bounded on two opposite sides by refractive surfaces of regular geometrical form having a common normal. These surfaces are usually either plane or spherical; non-spherical, or conic curvatures possessing no advantages for photographic purposes. In fig. 9 a series of lenses of various forms are shown in section. Each lens has either two spherical, or spherical and plane surfaces; and, as all centres of curvature are on the line PQ, which is also normal to every plane surface, that line is a common normal to all the surfaces, and to each lens.

The common normal to any lens is called the principal axis of the lens, and a ray of light coinciding with the principal axis passes through the lens without suffering any refraction, its angle of incidence being nil at each surface. When several lenses are employed in combination, their principal axes are made to coincide so that there is one common normal for all the lenses; this adjustment (a very delicate one to carry out) is called centring the lenses.

14. POSITIVE AND NEGATIVE LENSES.—The lenses shown in fig. 9. represent two classes, positive or convergent lenses (A, B, and C), and negative or divergent lenses (D, E, and F). The former are thicker in the centre than at the edges and the latter thickest at the edges. This is an essential distinction in simple single lenses, though it is not so with compound ones.

Figs. 1 to 4 (Secs. 3 and 4) showed the effect of

21

typical positive and negative lenses on a pencil of light
coming from a certain near source; we now consider the
case of the incident pencil being parallel, or having a
plane wavefront, as is the case when the source of light
is at an infinite distance from the lens. Under these
conditions—assuming the lens to be aplanatic (Sec. 5)—with
a positive lens (L_1 fig. 10) the emergent pencil is always
composed of converging rays and has a concave wavefront;
contracting on to a real focus. With a negative lens L_2
the emergent pencil is always divergent, and has a convex
wavefront expanding from a virtual focus Q. In fig. 10
rays are shown in full, and wavefronts in broken lines, and
the rays are continued to the virtual focus by dotted lines.

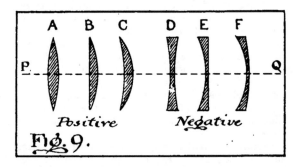

From these figures it is evident that with a positive lens
all non-axial rays suffer deviation towards the axis of the
light pencil, but with a negative lens they are deviated
from the axis. This is the characteristic distinction
between the two types of lenses, for, while positive lenses
with very near objects may fail to produce a real focus
they always produce positive deviation (towards the axis)
in non-axial rays; and negative lenses, which do not always
produce virtual foci, always produce negative deviation
away from the axis in non-axial rays. These conditions are
universal, whether the light pencils are "direct" (axial ray
coinciding with principal axis) or "oblique," and, as a result,
with positive lenses incident parallel rays are rendered
convergent, convergent incident rays more convergent, and

divergent rays either less divergent, parallel, or convergent. With negative lenses parallel rays become divergent, divergent rays more divergent, and convergent rays either less convergent, parallel, or divergent. The emergent rays come to a real focus if convergent, lead from a virtual focus if divergent, and come to no focus, or only to an infinitely distant one, if parallel. The formation of a focus of either a real or virtual type thus depends with either class of lenses on the nature of the incident pencil.

15. FORMS OF LENSES.—In fig. 9 six typical forms of

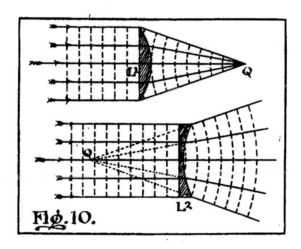

FIG. 10.

simple single glass lenses are shown. These are distinguished by the following names descriptive of their forms, surfaces, or properties.

Positive or Convergent Lenses.—

    A. A double convex lens; "symmetrical" if the surfaces are of the same curvatures, "crossed" if of different curvatures.

    B. A plano-convex or convexo-plane lens, according as we consider the light to be first incident on the plane or on the convex surface.

    C. A positive or convergent meniscus lens; or

convexo-concave or concavo-convex positive lens, also called a periscopic lens.

Negative or Divergent Lenses.—

D. A double concave lens, " symmetrical " or " crossed " according as the surfaces are of the same or different curvatures.

E. A plano-concave or concavo-plane lens.

F. A negative or divergent meniscus lens ; or concavo-convex or convexo-concave negative lens.

The above are, properly speaking, single lenses, but the term single is also applied to a combination of two or more lenses cemented together, or very slightly separated, to distinguish such a close combination from a double or triple combination, of widely separated lenses. Thus a " single " lens may be a single simple lens or a single combination of several simple lenses, and a doublet or triplet may consist of two or three separated simple lenses, or of two or three separated single combinations.

A doublet consisting of two separated simple lenses, or single combinations, is called a symmetrical doublet if the two lenses or combinations are similar in all respects. . If they vary it is non-symmetrical. If one single lens or combination is positive and the other negative, the doublet may be further distinguished as periscopic.* In fig. 11 some typical forms of single, double, and triple lenses are illustrated.

16. Lens Surfaces.—Simple lenses such as those shown in fig. 9, have two refractive surfaces, and it is sometimes convenient to look upon compound lenses as combinations of surfaces rather than of lenses.

The refractive surfaces of lenses may be classed as positive or negative according as non-axial rays are deviated to or from the principal axis. Speaking generally, a refractive surface between two media is positive when it is convex to the rarer medium, but negative when concave.

---

* See footnote to Sec. 5. Also see Sec. 95 in Chap. 10. The term " periscopic " being commonly applied to a single simple positive meniscus lens with one negative and one positive surface, is here applied to a doublet formed of one negative and one positive lens or single combination. A distinctive title for such doublets is desirable, but a better one might be devised.

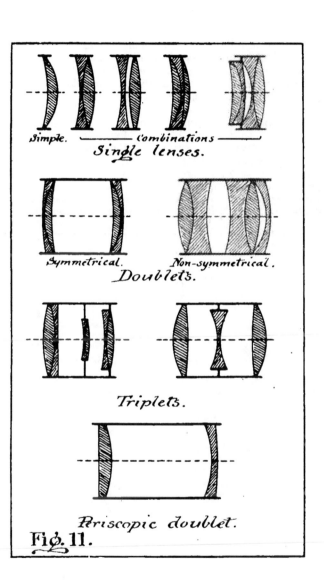

Simple. ——— Combinations ———

Single lenses.

Symmetrical.   Non-symmetrical.

Doublets.

Triplets.

Periscopic doublet.

Fig. 11.

Therefore, it follows that a double convex lens has two positive refractive surfaces, while a meniscus has one positive and one negative surface. By combining lenses together we can produce a positive combination possessing three or more surfaces. For example, lens A in fig. 12, has two positive surfaces. If we combine it with the negative lens F, as shown at a, the combination as a whole may be still positive, but it then has four refractive surfaces, three positive and one negative. If the adjacent curvatures of the lenses are of the same radius we may cement them together as at b, and we then have a positive lens with three refractive surfaces, if the component lenses are of different densities. If F is of denser material than A, the contact surface is negative, but if A is denser than F, the

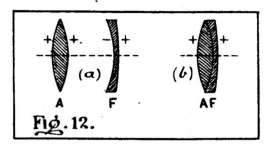

Fig. 12.

contact surface is positive, and we have three positive surfaces instead of two positive and one negative. The addition of a third lens cemented to A or F, and of different material, adds a fourth surface. If the third lens is separate we have five surfaces, and so a positive lens of any number of surfaces can be built up. We may then look upon the result, either as a combination of so many lenses, positive or negative, or as a combination of so many refractive positive or negative surfaces. To understand the purpose and effect of combining lenses it is advisable to adopt both points of view, as will be apparent later.

It should be observed that A and F must be of different densities to produce three surfaces when cemented; if of the same density the cemented contact surface is not a refractive surface (Sec. 10), and the lens as a whole has then only two surfaces. If the lenses are separated as at *a*, whatever the respective densities, there must be four surfaces.

17. FORMATION OF IMAGES.—In order that an object may be photographed it must be luminous; that is, it must either be a source of light or must reflect light emanating from some other source. The surface of the object may therefore be considered to consist of an infinite number of infinitely small luminous points, each of which emits light in all possible directions. By the employment of suitable optical appliances we select certain rays proceeding from each luminous point in the direction of the camera, and so control their course as to produce upon a screen, or sensitive surface, an image which may also be considered to consist of an infinite number of infinitely small points, each corresponding with one of the infinitely small luminous points in the object. For this purpose we employ either a pinhole, which only permits the passage of the few rays that are naturally travelling in the right direction, or a positive lens, which collects a number of rays travelling approximately in the right direction from the object point, and refracts them in such a way as to eventually bring them all to the proper image point.

To illustrate the formation of an image we need only consider two or three luminous points in the object and their corresponding image points, assuming that if these two or three image points are perfectly formed and correctly situated then the rest of the image lying between these points is also perfect and correct. The screen on which the image is received is in general a plane surface, and we assume that the object is also plane and parallel with the screen, both being intersected normally by a line which also passes normally through, or forms the principal axis cf, the pinhole or lens. It is desirable to take the intersection of the principal axis with the object plane as one of the selected object points.

18. PINHOLE IMAGE.—In fig. 13 *A* and *B* represent two infinitely small luminous points in the object. At *C* we place a screen containing a small pinhole (*h*) and a second screen at *D* to receive the image. Of all the light rays emanating from *A* only a few can pass through the pinhole,

the others being stopped by the screen *C.* The few rays
that do pass the hole will, however, continue straight on
until intercepted by the screen *D,* on which they form a
point of light at *a,* the size of the point varying with
the size of the pinhole. Similarly, a few rays from *B*
will also pass through the pinhole and form a second point
of light at *b.* As it is practically impossible to employ
an infinitely small pinhole the points of light *a* and *b* are
produced by straight rays forming narrow, slightly diverging
pencils of light; *a* and *b* are therefore discs rather than
points, and form a somewhat ill-defined inverted image of
A B. The definition is further affected by the optical
phenomenon called diffraction, but this matter need not
be now considered.*

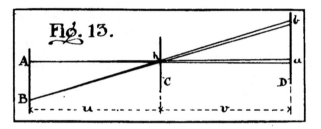

Fig. 13.

As the light rays suffer no deviation at the pinhole the
image, as a whole, geometrically corresponds with the object,
the latter being plane and parallel to the image screen.

19. SIZE OF PINHOLE IMAGE.—Assuming that the pinhole is capable of producing a well-defined image, it is
apparent that the linear dimensions of the image will vary
directly with the distance of the screen from the pinhole.
And as *AhB* and *ahb* (fig 13) are similar triangles, therefore
ab : *AB* : : *ha* : *Ah,* or the ratio of the image to the object,

---

* Diffraction is of considerable importance in the formation of
pinhole images, but has little practical effect on the lens image,
though it does play a part in its formation. It is an intricate
subject and can well be neglected in an elementary book on lenses
only. To understand diffraction, it is necessary to study minutely
the structure of a wavefront of light, a matter which was only
dealt with in very general terms in Chapter 1.

is equal to the ratio of the distance of the image from the pinhole to that of the object from the same point. If we let v represent the distance of the image, u that of the object, and R the ratio of image to object, then

$$R = \frac{v}{u} \quad \dots \quad \dots \quad \dots \quad (1).$$

20. LENS IMAGE.—If for the pinhole we substitute a positive lens (L), as shown in fig. 14, a similarly inverted image is again produced; but, as a much greater number of rays from the object points A and B pass through the lens than through the pinhole, the image is brighter; and, as all the transmitted rays converge on infinitely small image points a and b, the image is perfectly sharp. (We are of course assuming that the lens is aplanatic, and

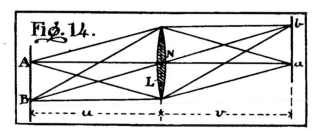

Fig. 14.

perfectly adapted to the purposes of photography; and this assumption must be maintained until we can consider aberration and its effects.) A lens thus produces a better defined image than a pinhole; and, as it also transmits more light, less exposure is necessary to produce a developable image.

21. CURVATURE OF FIELD.—Under the conditions assumed in Sec. 17, the lens must be capable of producing a plane image of a plane object; that is to say, all image points must lie in the plane of the screen. If this condition is not fulfilled the aberration known as curvature of the field exists. It must be particularly noted that both the object and image are assumed to be plane. A lens that has a curved image field for a plane object may produce a plane image from a curved object, but is not therefore to

be looked upon as a flat field lens. This is the third of
the three primary aberrations to which lenses are liable,
and which should all three be absent in the perfectly
adjusted or "corrected" photographic lens. In studying
the theoretical general action of lenses it is necessary to
assume in every case that the lens is aplanatic (Sec. 5),
achromatic (Sec. 7), and that it possesses flatness of field.

22. THIN AND THICK LENSES.—Fig. 14 may be considered to represent the manner in which the image is
formed with a lens of infinite thinness, if we disregard the
fact that such a lens is impracticable.   Waiving this
point, we may say that with a thin lens the image is produced by the agency of comparatively wide double pencils

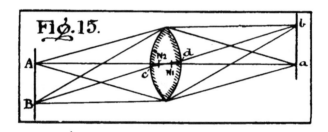

of light, the axial rays only of which are straight. As the
object and image points are situated on these axial rays,
which all intersect in the point N, the image geometrically
corresponds with the pinhole image, and is equally accurate,
while its size is governed by the same rule (Sec. 19).   In
fact a pinhole in the position of the point N will produce
a similar image, differing only in quality of definition.

All practicable lenses are, however, of appreciable
thickness, and a single thick lens produces an image by
the agency of double pencils of light with which the only
straight ray is that of the one direct pencil—*i.e.* the ray
coinciding with the principal axis of the lens (see *Aa*,
fig. 15). In oblique double pencils, such as *Bb*, there can
be no straight ray, but there is one axial ray ·(*Bcdb*),
which pursues parallel courses before and after refraction
(Sec. 10), and on these axial rays all image points are

situated. If we produce the rays *Bc* and *bd* to meet the
principal axis in the points N_2 and N_1, it will be apparent
that the image is formed on precisely the same geometrical
principles that govern its formation by the thin lens, the
only essential difference in the geometrical construction of
figs. 14 and 15 being the existence of the space N_2N_1 in
the latter figure.

In fig. 16 this matter is more clearly illustrated, only
axial rays being shown. BN_2 being parallel to N_1b, the
two diagrams are similar, excepting for the space N_2N_1.
The object and image being parallel, *ANB* and *aNb*, or
AN_2B and aN_1b, are similar triangles, and the scale of the

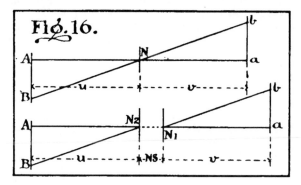

image is governed by the same principles as with a pinhole.
That is to say, $R = v/u$ if v and u are measured as indicated in fig. 16.

23. THE NODES OF A LENS.—The points N, N_1, and N_2,
illustrated in figs. 14 to 16, are called the nodes of the
lenses, the thin lens having one node and the thick lens
two. The separation of the two nodes (NS) is the nodal
space of the thick lens; and if in fig. 16 we assume that
the distance AN is equal to AN_2, and Na to N_1a, then,
the objects being the same, the images must be of equal
size; but the distance Aa with the thick lens is greater
than the distance Aa with the thin lens by NS, or the
amount of the nodal space N_2N_1. With a simple single
lens this nodal space is very approximately equal to

one-third the thickness of the lens, and is therefore a negligible quantity if the lens is thin, but its amount varies with compound lenses of various types.

In fig. 15 the nodes were found by producing the axial rays *Bc* and *bd* to meet the principal axis. In the ideally perfect lens the nodes are fixed points, and the axial rays of all oblique pencils would pass through the nodes if produced in the same way. The nodes are virtual points in the figure, but with some types of lenses one of them may be a real point; that is, axial rays may actually pass through it without any prolongation. In the example illustrated all incident axial rays will converge upon the point N_2, which is called the node of admission. All emergent axial rays will diverge from N_1, which is the node of emission. But if we reverse the lens, or look upon AB as an image of ab, these titles are reversed, and N_1 becomes the node of admission, while N_2 is that of emission.

These nodal points, or nodes, are sometimes termed principal points, or Gauss points. They can be shown to exist in every possible form of lens, simple or compound, that is capable of producing a perfect image, but their positions, relative to the lens and to each other, vary with different types of lenses.

24. THE THEORY OF THE EQUIVALENT LENS.—If we know the positions and separation of the nodes of a lens we can, as indicated in figs. 15 and 16, virtually trace the course of all oblique axial rays without paying any regard to the actual deviations produced in those rays by the various surfaces of which the lens is composed. Thus in fig. 15 the actual course of the refracted portion of the ray from c to d is of no consequence if the points N_1 and N_2 are fixed, and we may similarly disregard the actual course of an axial ray through a system of lenses of the most complicated nature if only the nodes are known. Therefore, we may, when considering the manner in which the image is formed, disregard all peculiarities of construction, and with a lens of the most complicated form proceed just as we should with a lens of the simplest possible character. Thus we may look upon the nodes of a complex doublet as being those of a simple lens "equivalent" to the

doublet in all respects. As, however, no simple single lens can practically produce a perfect image, we must adopt a conventional method of representing such an equivalent lens if we want to trace the course of non-axial rays, and this conventional representation is dependent on the Gauss theory.

25. THE GAUSS THEORY.—Assume that in fig. 17 we have a perfectly adjusted doublet formed of the two thin lenses C and D, the nodes of the doublet being at N_1 and N_2. Let BN_2N_1b represent the axial ray of an oblique pencil of light forming the image b of an object point B, as in the other diagrams. Through N_1 and N_2 draw the perpendicular lines shown, and assume them to represent sections of two parallel planes which are intersected normally by

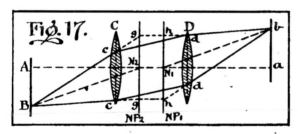

the principal axis Aa. These are called nodal planes, and are represented by the letters NP_1 and NP_2 in the diagram. Now any non-axial ray (Bc) starting from B and forming part of the pencil Bb, will be deviated by the lenses C and D at the points c and d, and will eventually arrive at b. Produce Bc and bd to meet the nodal planes in g and h. If then the lens is perfectly adjusted these two points will be opposite one another, and be equidistant from the principal axis,—that is, gh will be parallel to Aa. The course of any non-axial ray, even if exterior to the lenses, can be traced with the aid of the nodal planes if we know the positions of the object and image points, just as well as axial rays can be virtually traced through the nodal points. The rule being that all incident rays intersect the nodal plane of admission in a point normally opposite the point in the nodal plane of emission from which

3

emergent rays virtually start. The planes are considered to
be unlimited in extent.

These two parallel planes, together with the nodal points
and principal axis, thus form a conventional representation
of a perfectly adjusted lens, and if the equivalent lens
to a system of lenses be indicated in this manner, we can
disregard all constructional complications. If, however,
the system of lenses is not perfectly adjusted, or free from
aberration, this Gauss theory does not quite hold good;
but that is a matter for after consideration. It may be
noted that the effective aperture of the lens, or the diameter
of the incident pencil, is measured on the nodal plane of
admission.

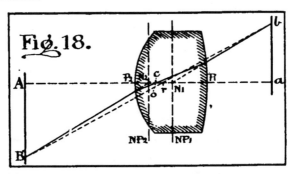

Fig. 18.

We have here only considered certain facts, the truth
of which can be proved under the Gauss theory. The
proofs of the existence of nodal points and nodal planes
which act in the way described are beyond our scope.
It must be pointed out that the Gauss theory is a modern
conception, and that in the older text-books no mention
will be found of either nodes or nodal planes. Under
the old theory, instead of two nodes, there was one optical,
or focal, centre, which under the new theory is a point
of very minor importance.

26. The Minor Points of a Lens.—Along the principal
axis of a lens there are (excluding the nodes) certain minor
points which require definition.

(a). *The poles* of a lens are the two points in which

the principal axis intersects the outer surfaces of the lens. The term pole is a convenient one, due to Professor Sylvanus Thompson (See P_2 and P_1 in fig. 18).

(b). *The rotary centre* is a point on the principal axis about which the lens may be rotated to a certain extent without producing any movement of the image. This point can be found by tentative experiment with a lens. On the diagram it is situated at the point where a straight line joining B and b intersects the principal axis (see r). The point is variable, but is always either between the nodes or at one of them. When the lens is focussed on an infinite distance the rotary centre coincides with the node of emission, but as the object is brought nearer the

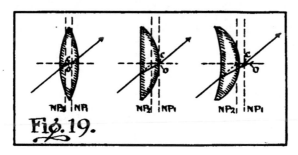

Fig. 19.

point moves towards the node of admission. The rotary centre is of little consequence excepting for the purpose of finding the nodes. A pinhole substituted for the lens in the position of the rotary centre will produce an image exactly similar to that formed by the lens, object and image being at a fixed distance apart.

(c). *Crossing-Point.* All oblique axial rays intersect one another, and also the principal axis, in one fixed point, the position of which varies according to the type of lens (see c in figs. 18 and 19). The crossing-point is always either at one of the nodes or between the two, but it does not necessarily coincide with the rotary centre (see fig. 18).

(d). *Optical Centre.* Just as all incident and emergent oblique axial rays meet at the nodes of admission and emission, so the refracted portions of all oblique axes meet, or will meet if produced, at one point. In the case of simple single lenses there is only one such point, as shown at *o* in figs. 18 and 19, and with such lenses that point is called the optical centre. It will be noticed that in the case of the meniscus lens the optical centre is virtual, outside the lens, and beyond the crossing-point ; in the other cases it is real and coincides with the crossing-point. With doublets we can also find a point which in certain respects corresponds to the optical centre of a single lens, but such a point is not usually recognised as an optical centre.

(*e*). *The focal centre* is a term applied in pre-Gauss days somewhat indiscriminately. It was intended to apply to the point from which all distances from the lens should be measured, but, as with single lenses the optical centre was taken, and with doublets the rotary centre (two quite distinct points), there is a good deal of confusion surrounding the term. Under the Gauss theory all measurements are made from the nodes (see fig. 16), which are the only points to which the term focal centre can now be applied.

It should be clearly understood that the rotary centre is the only variable point in the lens, while the nodes and optical centre are fixed points. The crossing-point is also fixed, but not independent of the others. It agrees with the optical centre if the latter is real, and with one of the nodes if the optical centre is virtual ; see fig. 19, in which the positions of the nodes are indicated by the nodal planes. The crossing-point is the most important of the minor points. The various points of a lens are frequently confused. The term "optical centre" is often applied to a node or to the rotary centre. Still more often is it applied to the point described in this book as the "crossing-point," though the two points exist separately in a meniscus lens. The optical centre is sometimes incorrectly defined and described, but correctly illustrated.

CHAPTER III.

27. The Principal Foci of a Lens.—When the object is at an infinite distance, so that the incident pencil is parallel, the focus of the emergent direct pencil is called a principal focus of the lens; and, as the lens may have either side turned towards the object, there are two principal foci, both situated on the principal axis and equidistant from the nodes of the lens. Thus, with the object on the side A of the positive lens L (fig. 20) the principal focus is on the principal axis at F_1, but with the object on the side B the principal focus is at F_2, the distances F_2N_2 and F_1N_1 being equal.

With a negative lens (fig. 21), the principal focus is on the same side as the object, and is virtual, and, the lens being again reversible, there are two principal foci (F_1 and F_2), and F_1N_1 is again equal to F_2N_2.

28. Focal Length and Focal Power.—The distance from the node of emission of a lens to its principal focus is called the focal length of the lens. Thus in figs. 20 and 21 the distance F_1N_1 or F_2N_2 is the focal length of either the negative or positive lens.

If we compare the effect of lenses on parallel pencils of equal diameter, or compare lenses of equal aperture (see Sec. 9) it will be noticed that the deviation produced in the outermost rays of the pencil is equal if the focal lengths are equal, while if the focal lengths differ the greatest deviation produces the shortest focal length. Thus, if in figs. 20 and 21 the incident parallel direct pencils are of the same diameter, and the angle F_1cb in fig. 20

is equal to F_1ca in fig. 21, then the focal lengths F_1N_1 are equal; but if F_1cb is greater than F_1ca the focal length of the positive lens must be less than that of the negative lens. Short focal length thus denotes that the lens has the power of producing great deviation, or is of great "focal power," and with very narrow pencils the focal power of a lens may be considered to vary inversely with its focal length. If, therefore, one lens has twice the focal length of another, it has only half the focal

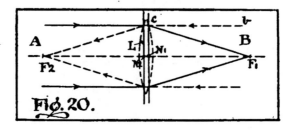

Fig. 20.

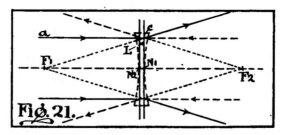

Fig. 21.

power; or if we represent the focal lengths of two lenses by f_1 and f_2, their focal powers are in the ratio of $1/f_1 : 1/f_2$. The greater the focal power the greater is the curvature of the emergent wavefront, and with the same two lenses the curvatures will be in the ratio of $1/f_1$ to $1/f_2$; thus the focal power may be taken to represent the curvature imprinted by the lens on the plane wavefront of the incident parallel pencil.

Focal length is a simple dimension that can be expressed in inches or centimetres (see Appendix, Table A). Focal power is a relative term, and conveys nothing definite unless we fix upon some particular unit of power. This unit is taken to be the focal power of a lens, the focal length of which equals one metre, and this unit of power is called a dioptrie. Thus a lens of half a metre focal length has a focal power of two dioptries, and so on. This method of expressing the power of lenses is in common use among oculists, while photographers always distinguish lenses by their focal lengths, using the expression "focal power" in a relative sense only (see Appendix, Table B).

29. CONJUGATE FOCI.—When the distance of the object is less than infinity, any object point and its corresponding image point are called conjugate foci. In practical photography we are concerned solely with one class of conjugate foci. We always use a positive lens, and the distance of the object is always greater than the focal length, and, under these conditions, the object focus is always on the opposite side of the lens and never nearer to it than the principal focus. To clearly understand conjugate foci it is, however, necessary to consider other cases, and to study the various classes of real and virtual foci produced under varying conditions.

In each of the following figs. (22 to 27) the points F_1 and F_2 are the two principal foci of the lens L, the nodal planes of which are shown in full lines, while its character (negative or positive) is indicated by dotted curvatures. In all cases we assume that the light travels from left to right.

With a Positive Lens.—If the object point is at an infinite distance the image is at F_1.

If the object is at P, farther from the lens than F_2 (see fig. 22), the image is at Q, and is real. P and Q are conjugate foci.

With the object at F_2, the image is at an infinite distance on the other side of the lens.

If the object P is between F_2 and the lens (fig. 23), the image is virtual and is at Q. P and Q are conjugate foci, Q being farther from the lens than P. In the particular case of P being half-way between F_2 and the lens, or at the semi-focus point, the conjugate focus Q is at F_2.

In the above cases the incident light is either parallel

or divergent; it may, however, be convergent on to a point
P behind the lens, as in fig. 24, in which case the conjugate focus is at Q, between F_1 and the lens. In this
case the object is virtual and the image real. If convergent on the principal focus F_1, Q is at the semi-focus,
half the focal length from F_1.

With a Negative Lens.—The object being at an infinite
distance a virtual focus is at F_1.

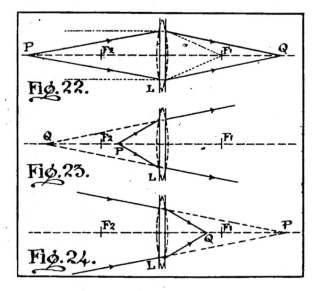

If the object is at P (fig. 25) the conjugate focus Q is
between the lens and the principal focus F_1.

If the object is at the principal focus F_1, the virtual
image Q is half-way between the principal focus and the
lens, or at the semi-focus.

If the incident pencil is convergent on to a point P
beyond the lens, but between it and its principal focus
F_2, a real image Q is formed at a greater distance
from the lens (fig. 26). P then represents a virtual
object.

If P is half-way between the lens and F_2, or at the semi-focus, the real image is at F_2.

If P is at F_2 the image is at an infinite distance.

If P is at a finite distance beyond F_2 the image is virtual, and is at Q (fig. 27) on the incident side of the lens, and farther from it than F_1. In this case P and Q are both virtual points.

With either class of lens any movement of the object

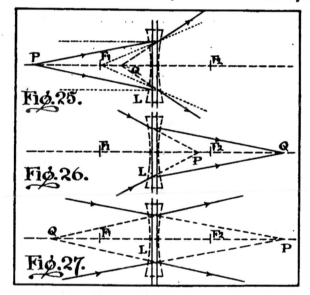

point is accompanied by a movement in the same direction of the conjugate image point.

30. CONJUGATE FOCAL DISTANCES.—The distance of the object measured from the node of admission, and that of the conjugate image focus measured from the node of emission are conjugate focal distances, which are always connected by a certain formula.

Let u represent the distance of the object, v that of the image, and f the focal length of the lens; then, with a positive lens, so long as the conditions illustrated in fig. 22, or the ordinary conditions of photography, are fulfilled,

$$\frac{1}{v} + \frac{1}{u} = \frac{1}{f} \quad \ldots \quad \ldots \quad \ldots \text{(2)}.$$

Knowing the values of two of the terms u, v, and f, the other can be easily found, either from the above fundamental equation, or from one of the following variations :

$$f = \frac{vu}{v + u} \quad \ldots \quad \ldots \quad \ldots \text{(3)}$$

$$u = \frac{fv}{v - f} \quad \ldots \quad \ldots \quad \ldots \text{(4)}$$

$$v = \frac{fu}{u - f} \quad \ldots \quad \ldots \quad \ldots \text{(5)}.$$

The conditions under which the above formulæ, as they stand, hold good, must be carefully noted ; under any other conditions the following convention with regard to the signs must be observed.

31. POPULAR SIGN CONVENTION. — Under the above-mentioned conditions all the focal points to which the distances v, u, and f relate are real, and the distances are positive in formula 2. Under other (non-photographic) conditions, one or more of the focal points might be virtual, in which case the corresponding distances would be negative. Briefly stated, we adopt the convention that the distance of a real focus is positive, while that of a virtual focus is negative, and from this it follows that

f is positive with a positive lens and negative with a negative lens.

v is positive so long as a real image is formed, and negative when the image is virtual.

u is positive so long as the incident pencil of light is divergent from a real source, and negative when the incident pencil is convergent on to a virtual source.

Applying the formulæ to the various cases illustrated in figs. 22 to 27, under this popular convention, in fig. 22, representing the conditions under which a photograph is taken, all distances are positive.

In 23 v is negative, while u and f are positive.

In 24 u is negative, and v and f positive.

In 25 v and f are both negative, u being positive.

In 26 u and f are negative, and v positive.

In 27 u, v, and f are all three negative.

Any problem relating to conjugate foci can be worked out by the formulæ given if the signs are changed in the case of any distance relating to a virtual focus. If in any case the result is a negative quantity, we know that the distance found relates to a virtual point, and, therefore, that the conditions are non-photographic. From formula 5 it is manifest that if u is less than f, the resultant value of v is negative, and the image is virtual. To give a real image, u must be not only positive but greater in value than f. Further, it may be noted that when these conditions are fulfilled, v is also greater than f.

32. THE STANDARD SIGN CONVENTION.—As misconceptions frequently arise from confusing sign conventions, it is advisable to explain the convention that is generally adopted in standard text-books upon general optics.

All distances being measured from the lens to the focal point, any distance measured in the same direction as that of the incident light is negative, while any distance measured in an opposite direction to that of the incident light is positive.

This is a very complete definition, but it is somewhat confusing to the beginner. It may perhaps be summed up as implying that the length of a convergent pencil of light is negative, while that of a divergent one is positive; but it is instructive to look at the matter from a physical point of view.

If we consider that the curvature of the wavefront of an incident or emergent pencil varies inversely with the distances of the object or image, then, if the distances are in the ratio of u to v, the curvatures are in that of $1/u$ to $1/v$.

When an incident pencil with a wavefront of a certain curvature falls upon a lens of a certain focal power (see Sec. 28), the curvature of the wavefront of the emergent pencil is equal to the sum of the curvature of the incident wavefront and the focal power, which also represents a curvature: thus; $1/v = 1/u + 1/f$. When, however, the focal power represents a curvature of an opposite nature to that of the incident pencil, one neutralises the other to a certain extent, and a universally applicable formula can be found if we adopt the convention that a convex wave-front is positive, while a concave one is negative. This renders the focal power of a positive lens negative, while that of a negative lens is positive. If then we have a divergent pencil incident on a negative lens, both the incident and emergent pencils have positive curvatures, thus all the terms are positive and the formula mentioned above applies as it stands, though it is generally transposed into $1/v - 1/u = 1/f$.

With a positive lens giving a real focus the focal power is

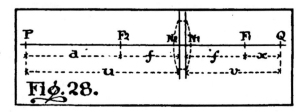

FIG. 28.

negative, while the emergent wavefront is concave, hence we have :

$$\frac{1}{-v} - \frac{1}{u} = \frac{1}{-f} \; ; \; \text{or,} \; \frac{1}{v} + \frac{1}{u} = \frac{1}{f}$$

which is the same formula as that given under the popular convention. It is the conventions only, not the formulæ, that differ, and while under the standard convention the fundamental formula is the one relating only to negative lenses, under the popular convention it is that relating to positive lenses working under ordinary photographic conditions.

In studying general optics the adoption of the standard convention is imperative, but the popular convention is preferred in this book as it is more easily understood, and is applicable to all the problems that photographers meet with in connection with lenses.

33. EXTRA-FOCAL DISTANCES.—As both v and u must be greater than f when a real image is produced with a positive lens, a pair of conjugate foci P and Q (fig. 28) must be outside the principal foci F_1 and F_2. The distances u and v of these conjugate foci, measured from the nodes of the lens, are called focal distances; but we may measure the distances of P and Q from the principal foci F_1 and F_2, and distinguish them as the extra-focal distances d and x. This method of measuring has advantages inasmuch as the formula connecting the extra-focal distances is simpler than that given for focal distances. If in formula 2 we substitute $d+f$ for u, and $f+x$ for v, we have

$$dx = f^2 \quad \dots \quad \dots \quad \dots \quad (6).$$

The fundamental formulæ for conjugate focal and extra-focal distances are of constant use in connection with lenses, and will be frequently referred to. The following formula expresses the relationship between focal and extra-focal distances and scale of image:

$$\frac{v}{u} = \frac{f}{d} = \frac{x}{f} = R \quad \dots \quad \dots \quad \dots \quad (7).$$

34. CONJUGATE SYMMETRIC FOCI. From the formula $1/u + 1/v = 1/f$ it is apparent that when u equals v they each equal $2f$; that is to say, when the object is at a distance of two focal lengths from a positive lens, the image is at an equal distance on the other side. The image is then exactly the same size as the object (see Secs. 19 and 22), and thus the term symmetric foci (due to Professor Sylvanus Thompson) is very suitable. It is also useful, as these particular conjugate foci have often to be specially referred to. There are no symmetric foci to a negative lens.

35. CONJUGATE PRINCIPAL FOCI.—If two lenses are used in combination the principal foci of the individual component lenses are conjugate foci, though the corresponding conjugate focal distances are not necessarily equal to the focal lengths. It is apparent that if the object is at the principal focus of the first lens the pencil emergent from that lens and incident on the second is a parallel pencil, hence the image is at the principal focus of the second lens.

36. THE CARDINAL POINTS OF A LENS.—We have considered several particular points situated on the principal axis of a positive lens, but the two nodes and the two principal foci are so essentially important that they may be looked upon as cardinal points. The principal, foci are always equidistant from their respective nodes but the relative positions of the nodes are liable to variations. Fig. 29 shows four different possible relative positions for the cardinal points. In each case the focal lengths N_1F_1 and N_2F_2 are equal, but in case A the nodes are separated so that the distance from F_2 to F_1 equals $f+NS+f$. In case B the nodes are coincident, and $F_1F_2 = 2f$. In case C the nodes are crossed, so that $F_1F_2 = f+f-NS$. In case

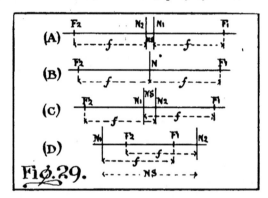

Fig. 29.

D the nodes are crossed, but outside the principal foci; F_1F_2 still being equal to $f+f-NS$.

Separated nodes are most common, and fig. 29A may be taken to illustrate the cardinal points of a thick simple single lens, or of a doublet of two thick lenses, or of the majority of compound single lenses. Coincident nodes are rare, and fig. 29B may illustrate the points of a hypothetical infinitely thin single lens, or of a doublet of two lenses of medium thickness. Crossed nodes, as in fig. 29C, exist with some forms of compound single lenses, and with doublets of thin lenses, but fig. 29D illustrates a very rare case, only met with in microscope lenses.

Though coincident nodes are unusual, it often happens that separated or crossed nodes are so close together that for all practical purposes they may be looked upon as coincident. Sometimes, however, this is so far from being the case, that the nodal space becomes a very important factor in calculating distances. With single simple lenses the nodes must be separated, and the nodal space is very approximately equal to one-third the thickness of the lens. The nodes may be crossed with compound single lenses.

With crossed nodes the nodal space has to be deducted from the sum of two focal distances to find the actual distance from object to image, and the space may be looked upon as negative. With separated nodes the space may be considered positive.

37. THE POSITIONS OF THE NODES.—The positions of the

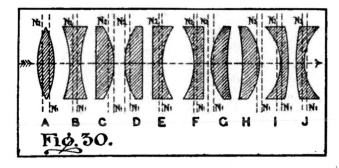

Fig. 30.

nodes of a single lens, relative to the lens, vary in different types of lenses, and in fig. 30 a series of typical single positive and negative lenses are shown. The light is assumed to be passing in the direction of the arrow, and the nodal planes of admission and emission are marked N_2 and N_1 above and below the lenses. When the curvatures are unequal the nodes are nearer the side of greatest curvature, one node being on the curved surface with a plano lens, and outside the lens, or "free," with a meniscus. When a node is on the surface, it coincides with both the crossing-point and the optical centre. When outside the lens it coincides with the crossing-point only (see Sec. 26).

With combinations of lenses there is a very much greater

variety of possible positions for the nodes. They may
both be not only outside the lens, but a very long way
outside. The telephoto lens is specially designed with a
view to throwing the nodes so far outside and in front
of the lens as to produce the effect of a lens of very long
focal length, though the lens itself is comparatively close
to the plate. On the other hand, with the type of com
bination known as a single landscape lens, the nodes are
between the lens and the plate, and a greater extension
of camera is therefore required than would be necessary
if the nodes were in front of the lens, or within it, as
is the case with the ordinary doublet.

With separated photographic combinations of the doublet
form, if the lenses are both positive or both negative,

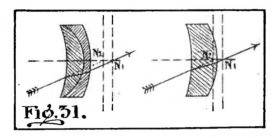

Fi⌀.31.

the nodes (which may be separated, crossed, or coincident),
are between them, but nearest to the lens of greatest focal
power. If one lens is positive and one negative, the nodes
(usually separated) are free, or outside the combination
altogether, being beyond the positive lens if the combination as a whole is positive, and beyond the negative lens
if the combination is negative.

With cemented or close combinations the positions of
the nodes are somewhat similar to those which they would
occupy in the case of a simple lens of the same outward
form, excepting that the nodes may be crossed or possibly
coincident; and, in the case of a meniscus, may both be
free, instead of one being free, and one inside the lens.
With the single meniscus combination of an achromatic
landscape, or rectilinear, both nodes are usually free and

beyond the convex surface, as shown in fig. 31, in which an achromatic meniscus is compared with a single meniscus.

Mr. T. R. Dallmeyer, in the first Traill Taylor Memorial Lecture, stated that in the stigmatic of 6·4 ins. focal length, the nodes " of the front combination are slightly crossed, near together and about six-tenths of an inch in front ; in the back combination they are not crossed near together, and as much as one and a quarter inches behind the lens." These are exceptional examples of single combinations, but many variations are possible.

38. EQUIVALENT LENSES.—The theoretical equivalent lens to a combination has already been defined (Sec 24), but we may describe two separate lenses, capable of producing similar effects under all similar conditions, as equivalent to one another. With two such lenses the cardinal points are exactly the same ; that is to say, the nodal spaces are equal and of the same sign, and the focal lengths are equal. Equal focal length alone does not render the lenses truly equivalent ; the nodal spaces must also be equal if the lenses are to produce exactly similar effects at all distances. On the other hand, equivalency does not necessarily imply that the positions of the cardinal points relative to the lens are the same in both cases ; in this respect the lenses may differ widely, and they may have no outward resemblance to one another, even though they are strictly equivalent. It need hardly be added that to be truly equivalent, lenses should be equally free from aberration.

Strictly equivalent lenses are necessary in a stereoscopic camera, as lenses of equal focal length but of unequal nodal spaces produce similar images only when the object is at an infinite distance. With nearer objects the images vary in size.

CHAPTER IV.

COMBINING LENSES.

39. EFFECT OF COMBINING LENSES.—When lenses are combined to form a system the focal length of the whole combination depends upon the focal powers of the component lenses, and also upon whether they are in nodal contact or nodally separated. The positions of the cardinal points of the combination depend on the same conditions, and also on the nodal spaces of the component lenses. Lenses are combined mainly for the purpose of producing a system free from aberration, but sometimes we combine them for the express purpose of altering focal length, and the effect produced upon focal length and the cardinal points is the matter of present consideration. First, however, we must consider the meaning of nodal contact between two lenses, which is a matter very liable to be misunderstood, and demands particular explanation.

40. NODAL CONTACT AND SEPARATION.—A condition of perfect nodal contact is secured between two lenses when the node of emission of the front lens (the one nearest the incident light) coincides with the node of admission of the back lens (the one nearest the image). When the lenses are not thus in contact the distance between the two nodes mentioned represents the separation of the lenses. In some cases the node of emission of the front lens may be behind the node of admission of the back lens, which case is distinguished as crossed, or negative separation. It must be clearly understood that nodal contact does not necessarily involve the touching of the lenses, it is, in fact, an unusual condition even with cemented lenses, and there

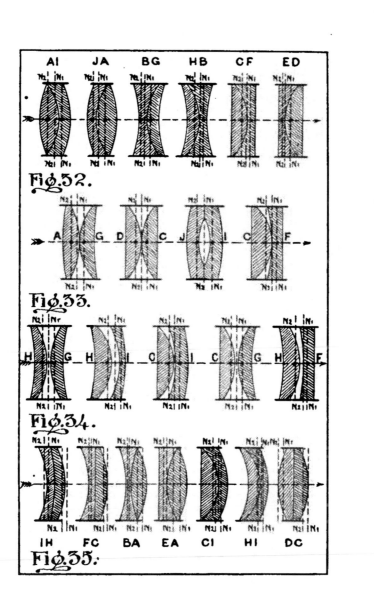

AI   JA   BG   HB   CF   ED

Fig.52.

Fig.33.

Fig.34.

IH   FC   BA   EA   CI   HI   DC

Fig.35.

are many forms of lenses that cannot possibly be placed in nodal contact.

Figs. 32 to 35 show various combinations of two lenses, each marked to correspond with typical lenses shown in fig. 30. The nodal planes of the front lenses are marked above the axis, those of the back lenses below the axis. The direction of the light is shown by the arrow.

Fig. 32 practically includes all the possible forms of cemented double combinations of positive and negative lenses with which the condition of nodal contact can be secured. It is impossible to cement two positive or two negative lenses in nodal contact.

Fig. 33 gives a few examples of lenses that touch and are in contact, but cannot be cemented. Pairs of positive or of negative lenses are possible in this case.

Fig. 34 shows some lenses in contact without touching; a condition that cannot well be fulfilled with a pair of negative lenses.

Fig. 35 gives a few only out of a great variety of possible cemented combinations in which the condition of contact is not secured at all. Many of these are to be found in photographic lenses. *CI* and *HI* are examples of crossed or negative separation. In the rest the separation is positive.

It will be noticed from these figures that nodal contact cannot be secured when each node is within its respective lens. One or both nodes must be free to a certain extent dependent on the form of the lens. The same conditions hold good when one of the two lenses is a doublet; one node must be sufficiently free to reach the other. In the case of a doublet a free node must be outside, not between the lenses composing the doublet. No form of simple single lens can be placed in contact with an ordinary doublet consisting of two positive combinations, though nodal contact can be readily secured if the doublet is of the periscopic form, as it then has a free node.

41. FOCAL LENGTH OF COMBINATION.—If to a positive lens of focal length f_1 we add another positive lens of focal length f_2, and nodal contact is secured, then the focal power of the combination is equal to the sum of

the focal powers of the component lenses. Let F equal the focal length of the combination. Then $1/F$ equals its focal power and,

$$\frac{1}{F} = \frac{1}{f_1} + \frac{1}{f_2} \quad \dots \quad \dots \quad \dots \quad (8)$$

or,

$$F = \frac{f_1 f_2}{f_1 + f_2} \quad \dots \quad . \quad \dots \quad \dots \quad (9).$$

If the lenses are not in contact, but nodally separated by a positive distance equal to a, then

$$\frac{1}{F} = \frac{1}{f_1} + \frac{1}{f_2} - \frac{a}{f_1 f_2} \quad \dots \quad \dots \quad (10)$$

or,

$$F = \frac{f_1 f_2}{f_1 + f_2 - a} \quad \dots \quad \dots \quad \dots \quad (11).$$

By adding a positive lens to a positive we increase focal power, or diminish focal length, and the less the separation the shorter is the focal length.

By adding a negative lens to a positive we reduce focal power or increase focal length, and the less the separation the greater is the focal length.

In either case the nearer the second lens is to the first the greater is its effect upon focal length.

The formulæ given apply to the case of negative lenses if a *minus* sign is prefixed to the term representing the focal length or power of the negative lens. If the nodal separation is crossed or negative the sign prefixed to a is changed.

When the resultant value of F is positive the combination is positive, or has a real focus. If the result is negative the combination has a virtual focus, or is negative. If the result is infinite, there is no focus; that is to say, one lens has neutralised the other. To preserve a real focus in a combination of negative and positive lenses, the negative lens must be of less power or greater focal length than the other, if they are in nodal contact. If separated the negative lens may be of greater focal power, provided the separation is greater than the difference between the focal lengths. Thus, suppose we combine a

positive lens of 6 ins. focal length with a negative lens
of 3 ins. focal length. Placing them in contact we have
a negative combination of 6 ins. focal length. With
a separation of 3 ins. the focal length is infinite, or
the combination is neutral. With a separation of
4 ins. we have a positive combination of 18 ins. focal
length.

It should be noted that the formulæ only apply to
combinations of distinct lenses. They do not apply if
one lens is placed inside the other, as it may be when one
of the lenses is itself a separated combination.

42. NODES OF A COMBINATION.—When two lenses are
in nodal contact the other two nodes form the nodes of

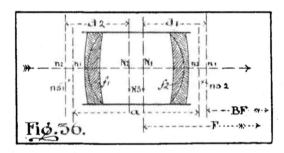

Fig. 36.

the combination, as shown in figs. 32, 33, and 34, where
the nodes of the combination are marked by black dots.
If nodal contact is not secured the nodes take different
positions.

As an example we will take a combination of two
positive lenses, forming a doublet as shown in fig. 36.
The position of the nodes of this combination can be
calculated if we know those of the single lenses. In the
following formulæ, d_2 is the distance of the node of
admission of the combination from the node of admission
of the front single lens (which may be either a simple
lens or compound as shown), and d_1 is the distance of the
node of emission of the combination from the node of
emission of the back lens. The other letters are the same
as in formulæ 8-11, f_1 being the focal length of the front

and f_2 of the back lens, while a is the separation of the two lenses.

$$d_2 = \frac{af_1}{f_1 + f_2 - a} = \frac{aF}{f_2} \quad \ldots \quad \ldots \quad \ldots \quad (12)$$

$$d_1 = \frac{af_2}{f_1 + f_2 - a} = \frac{aF}{f_1} = d_2 \times \frac{f_2}{f_1} \quad \ldots \quad (13).$$

If negative lenses are involved, or the separation a is crossed, the signs must be varied as before explained. If the result is positive, d_2 is measured towards the image and d_1 towards the object, as in fig. 36. If either result is negative, the distance is measured in the opposite

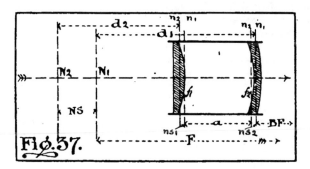

FIG. 37.

direction. Thus, in the case of a telephoto lens, illustrated by the periscopic doublet fig. 37, the back lens is negative and the front positive; a is greater than $f_1 - f_2$, hence d_2 becomes negative and d_1 positive, both are therefore measured in the same direction, towards the object.

To find the separation of the nodes, or the nodal space of the doublet, we must know the nodal spaces of the component lenses. Let ns_1 and ns_2 be the nodal spaces of the front and back lenses respectively, and NS that of the combination (see figs. 36 and 37). Then

$$NS = ns_1 + ns_2 - \frac{a^2}{f_1 + f_2 - a} \quad \ldots \quad \ldots \quad \ldots \quad (14).$$

If the result is negative the nodes are crossed.

In some cases the values of ns_1 and ns_2 are so small

that they may be neglected. This is especially the case with the telephoto lens with which the value of NS may be many feet; but when NS is very small, ns_1 and ns_2 are of importance. If they are neglected in the case of an ordinary rectilinear combination, a negative value for NS is always obtained, whereas with the majority of such combinations it is positive.

43. BACK-FOCUS OF COMBINATION.—This term is used to denote the distance between the image and the node of emission of the nearest single lens of the combination (see BF in figs. 36 and 37). It is not a correct term, as a focus is a point and not a dimension, but it is a useful expression. The back-focus is a very important dimension with the telephoto lens, though not of much consequence with other forms of lenses. As a rule it indicates, more or less accurately, the extension of camera required. With a rectilinear or single landscape lens, the extension measured to the lens flange, or face of camera front, is usually less than an inch greater than the back-focus, but with telephoto lenses the extension is from 2 to 6 ins. greater. The back-focus is less than the focal length with all combinations, excepting such as have their nodes behind the back lens. The ordinary type of single landscape lens is an example. Using the same symbols as in formula 11 we can find the back-focus, or BF, from the general formula :

$$BF = \frac{f_2(f_1 - a)}{f_1 + f_2 - a} \quad \ldots \quad \ldots \quad \ldots \quad (15).$$

This is equal to the difference between formulæ 11 and 13, or to $F - d_1$ in figs. 36 and 37.

In the case of a telephoto lens, with which this formula is most often required, a negative sign has of course to be prefixed to f_2.

44. COMBINATIONS OF MORE THAN TWO LENSES.—The formulæ given, and the principles laid down, with regard to combinations of two lenses apply equally well to combinations of three or more lenses, if we take the lenses in pairs, and remember that the formulæ only apply when combining distinct lenses, or lens systems. Thus, if we have three lenses in series A, B, and C, we can first find

the focal length and nodes of a doublet consisting of A and B, and then find similar particulars for a combination of C with the equivalent lens to A and B. Or we can reverse the procedure; first combine B with C, and then the result with A. We cannot, however, combine the centre lens B with the equivalent lens to A and C.

With a series of four lenses, A, B, C, and D, we can proceed in two ways. We may combine A with B, and also C with D, and then combine the results; or we can combine A with B, the result with C, and this result with D. It may be useful to give formulæ for the direct combination of three lenses A, B, and C, separated by intervals

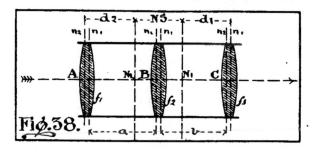

Fig. 38.

equal to a and b, and of focal lengths f_1, f_2, and f_3, as shown in fig. 38.

$$F = \frac{f_1 f_2 f_3}{f_2(f_1 - a) + (f_2 - b)(f_1 + f_2 - a)} \quad \cdots \quad \cdots \quad (16)$$

$$d_1 = \frac{bf_2 + a(f_2 + f_3 - b)}{f_2(f_1 - a) + (f_2 - b)(f_1 + f_2 - a)} \quad \cdots \quad \cdots \quad (17)$$

$$d_2 = \frac{af_2 + b(f_1 + f_2 - a)}{f_2(f_1 - a) + (f_3 - b)(f_1 + f_2 - a)} \quad \cdots \quad \cdots \quad (18).$$

45. Supplementary Lenses.—It is sometimes desirable to add a supplementary lens to an existing combination for the purpose of increasing or diminishing its focal length. The formulæ previously given are sufficient to meet all requirements, but, as sometimes their application is imperfectly understood, it is as well to illustrate some actual cases. Mistakes most usually occurring in connection with the matter of separation, attention is more particularly directed to that point. We may assume that the original combination is adjusted so as to produce an image free from the effects of aberration, and as it is essential that this adjustment shall not be appreciably disturbed by the addition of the extra lens, the supplementary lens must be thin with practically only one node and of weak focal power. We may add also that it is generally safer to use a negative lens for the purpose of increasing focal length than to add a positive lens to reduce focal length, and that some consideration should be given to the form of the supplementary lens.

Adding Supplementary Lens to Single Landscape Lens.— Suppose we want to add a supplementary lens B to a single

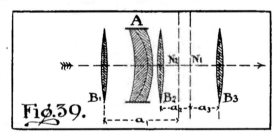

Fig.39.

landscape lens A, as shown in fig. 39. Landscape lenses are of the meniscus form, and present their concave surface to the object, hence their nodes are usually behind, as shown at N_2 and N_1.

If the supplementary lens (which should be of meniscus or plano form) is placed at B_1 (near the stop of the landscape lens) it is in front of A ; the distance of separation is measured to N_2, is positive, and equals a_1.

If B is at B_2 it is behind A, but its node of admission is in front of N_1 (the node of emission of A), hence the separation is negative and equals a_2. In many cases the amount of separation may be practically negligible, but the example is a good illustration of negative separation (see Sec. 40). If B is at B_3 it is behind A, and its node is also behind N_1, hence the separation a_3 is positive.

Adding Supplementary Lens outside Doublet.—Fig. 40

represents a doublet composed of two positive single
combinations A and B. The nodes of the doublet are
marked N_2 and N_1, and those of the component lenses n_2
and n_1. The supplementary lens C (preferably of plano
form) may be placed either in front of the doublet, at C_1, or
behind it, at C_2; and in either case the separation b_1, or
b_2, is positive. A minimum amount of separation exists
when C is close to the most powerful component lens

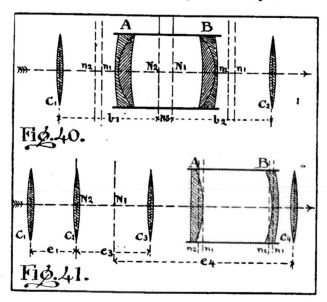

of the doublet, therefore in this position we secure the
nearest possible approach to nodal contact with the
doublet. If A and B are of equal focal length the minimum
separation of C is approximately half the extreme length
of the doublet.

With a periscopic doublet, such as that shown in
fig. 41, nodal contact can be secured by placing C in
position C_2, at the node of admission of the doublet; at
C_1 the separation equals e_1, and is positive; at C_3 the

separation equals e_3 and is negative; at C_4 the separation
equals e_4, and is positive.

Adding Supplementary Lens inside Doublet.—If the supplementary lens C is placed between the positive lenses
A and B in fig. 40, the ordinary formulæ no longer
apply, and to arrive exactly at the focal length of the
combination we must have all the data necessary to
determine the focal length of a triplet (see Sec. 44);
but the accurate result thus arrived at will not differ
to an appreciable extent from that obtained when the
lens C is placed outside and close to one of the component
lenses A, or B, if they are of approximately the same
focal length. Thus, when the supplementary lens is
inside the doublet it is generally sufficient to apply the usual
formulæ, taking the separation as equal to approximately
half the extreme length of the doublet. A double convex
or concave is the best form of supplementary lens to
use inside a doublet.

If the doublet is of the periscopic form, as in fig. 41,
we must work out the whole combination as a triplet, for
slight variations in the position of the lens C greatly
affect the result.

Use of Magnifiers.—We do not always add a supplementary lens for the express purpose of altering focal length,
though that is a necessary consequence. With cameras
that have no focussing arrangement, and with which the
focussing-screen is fixed at the principal focus of the lens,
any near object can be brought into focus on the screen
by adding in front of the lens a supplementary lens the
focal length of which is equal to the distance of the object.
The addition of this lens brings the near object into focus,
but does not materially alter the size of the image, hence
the term magnifier, which is commonly applied to
supplementary lenses when used in this way, is hardly a
happy one. The resultant focal length of the whole
combination can of course be found by the formulæ given,
but it is of little consequence, for, in the absence of any
focussing arrangement the only conjugate foci that we can
make use of are the principal foci of the two lenses, which
form the conjugate principal foci of the combination
(see Sec. 35).

CHAPTER V.

46. THE PRIMARY ABERRATIONS.—As before explained, the ideal photographic image of a plane object may be considered to be formed of an infinite number of infinitely small points, each being the image of a corresponding small point in the object, all such image points being situated in a plane parallel to that of the object, and both planes being intersected normally by the principal axis of the lens. The essential requirements of the ideal photographic image therefore are,

1. Perfect formation of the image points.
2. Perfect complaneity of all image points.
3. Correct relative situation of each image point.

The presence of aberration is denoted by non-compliance with one or more of these requirements.* They are, however, all fulfilled with any simple positive lens, provided that the light is monochromatic, or of one colour only, that the pencils of light are infinitely narrow, and that oblique pencils are only inclined at infinitely small angles to the principal axis. In photography these conditions cannot be fulfilled: the light employed is compound; the production of sufficient exposure effect within a reasonable time necessitates the employment of wide pencils, or of large apertures; and pencils of a considerable degree of

---

* If these requirements are fulfilled the lens may be described as "collinear"; a term which implies that it is also "aplanatic," "achromatic," "stigmatic," or "anastigmatic," and "orthoscopic," or "rectilinear." From these terms the distinctive titles applied to particular lenses are in many cases derived, though a truly "collinear" lens has not yet been manufactured.

obliquity are necessary to the production of an image of any size.

The employment of wide pencils renders apparent the effects of spherical aberration; the light being compound, chromatic aberration appears; and the employment of pencils of considerable obliquity accentuates the effects of curvature of the field. Either of these three primary aberrations causes the production of blurred image points, and a consequent loss of definition.

47. SECONDARY ABERRATIONS.—These may be due to several causes.

1st. The primary aberrations become complicated under varying conditions, and produce distinctive effects, which are sometimes classed as separate aberrations, though they would be more properly described as secondary effects of the primary aberrations. For example, spherical aberration in an oblique pencil is complicated by two effects known as " coma " and " astigmatism "; and the latter causes complicated effects of curvature of the field.

2nd. The attempt to correct one form of aberration may introduce another secondary form. Thus, in modifying certain forms of aberration by the use of a stop or diaphragm, diaphragm distortion may be introduced.

3rd. Correction may be either incomplete, or carried too far; and in either case the remaining aberration may be classed as secondary.

48. PRINCIPLES OF CORRECTION.—There are three general principles of correction.—*1st,* The elimination of aberrated rays; *2nd,* Diminution of effect of blur; *3rd,* Compensation of the aberration.

The first principle is carried out by adjusting a stop or diaphragm to cut out all rays excepting such as come to foci at (or very near) the proper points. This generally requires careful adjustment of the position of the diaphragm relative to the lens, and is a matter for the optician to settle.

The second principle, diminution of effect, is applied by reducing the diameter of the aperture of the diaphragm. This reduces the effective aperture of the lens, the diameter of the light pencil, and the size of the blur at the focus. This is a matter under the control of the photographer, and a very small aperture will practically obviate, though it may not actually correct, the effects of any form of aberration excepting such as its use may introduce.

The third principle, compensation, is the most important, as it is carried out independently of the aperture and does not interfere with rapidity. Aberration is compensated by combining lenses or refractive surfaces that individually produce opposite forms of the same aberration, and that in combination neutralise each other's effects. If the aberration varies to any considerable extent with the form of the lens, two positive lenses of opposite forms may com-

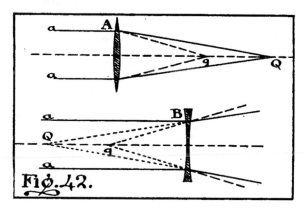

Fig. 42.

pensate each other; but if it varies more especially with the power of the lens, lenses of opposite (positive and negative) powers are combined.

49. POSITIVE AND NEGATIVE ABERRATION.—If we compare the aberration of a positive lens with the similar aberration of a negative lens acting under the same conditions, it will be found that while the effects produced at the foci are similar, the emergent pencils are affected in exactly opposite manners; this is due to the fact that while in the one case the focus and emergent pencil are on the same side of the lens, in the other they are on opposite sides.

Suppose the aberration with a positive lens *A* (fig. 42)

is such that a certain pair of rays *aa* come to too near a focus (to *q* instead of *Q*), or are too convergent; then with a negative lens *B* the same pair of rays have a virtual focus which is also too near the lens, which renders them too divergent; hence the ultimate effects are opposite, and if the two lenses are combined, the excessive convergency given by the one may be neutralised by the excessive divergency given by the other. Similar conditions prevail with positive and negative surfaces.

To perfectly compensate aberration the positive aberration of the one lens must be exactly neutralised by the negative aberration of the other, but, at the same time, there must be an excess of positive focal. power to preserve a real focus. It is therefore necessary to very carefully adjust the conditions that affect the extent of the aberration.

It should be noted that negative aberration can only be observed on the focussing-screen with the aid of an over-compensated positive combination. Over correction introduces negative aberration, just as under correction leaves a residue of positive aberration.

50. GENERAL PRINCIPLES OF COMPENSATION.—If the two lenses are separate the required adjustment can be made by varying the materials and curvatures of each, and the degree of separation between them, and additional control is obtained by multiplying the number of lenses or surfaces. If, however, the two lenses are cemented in contact so that the combination only possesses three surfaces, the power of correction is somewhat limited. For example, suppose *A* and *B* (fig. 42) to be cemented; and the light to be monochromatic. *A* must be of greater focal power than *B* to preserve a real focus, and the two lenses must be of different material, otherwise the contact surface will be neutral and we shall have a simple positive lens of two surfaces only and possessing positive aberration. If, however, *B* is of greater refractive power than *A*, the contact surface is negative and gives negative aberration, the amount of which can be adjusted by suitable selection of materials to just counteract the positive aberration of the outer surfaces, *provided the latter is not excessive.* Similarly, with compound light, if *B* is of greater dispersive power than *A*, the contact surface giving negative

dispersion can be adjusted to counteract the positive dispersion of the outer surfaces.

If the positive and negative lenses are separate, and perfectly adjusted to one another, a reduction of the amount of separation produces too much negative effect, and introduces over-corrected aberration of a negative character. If, on the other hand, the separation is increased, the effect of the negative lens is diminished, and under correction results.

When lenses are separated it is not in all cases absolutely necessary that they should be of opposite power, thus in a telescopic eye-piece two separated positive lenses may counteract each other's spherical or chromatic aberration ; but in photographic lenses these two aberrations are corrected by the employment of compensating negative lenses, the result being only slightly affected by the separation of the positive combinations forming a doublet. Positive compensating lenses are in general only employed for correcting particular secondary effects of aberration, such as coma and distortion.

Compensation is the most important principle of correction, for the more use we can make of it the less are we dependent on the diaphragm, and the greater is the rapidity and general usefulness of the lens. In the ordinary landscape lens so much depends on the diaphragm that a small aperture has to be used under almost all circumstances. With the ordinary rectilinear doublet a larger relative aperture can be used; but much still depends on the diaphragm, and while such a lens is faster than a single lens of the same focal power it is much slower than the "anastigmat," in which the diaphragm is responsible in only a slight degree for the correction of aberration.

Portrait lenses are the quickest in use, but large apertures are employed with these, not because the lenses are better compensated, but because the presence of certain aberrations is of less consequence in the particular case of portraiture. If employed for other purposes the aperture has to be reduced considerably, and other forms of lenses will serve fairly well for portraiture if their apertures are greatly increased. It is simply a matter of compromise, and the science of optics is, unfortunately, not yet sufficiently

far advanced to render compromises unnecessary. A lens
that will perfectly fulfil every possible condition has not
yet been designed. If perfect for copying a near object it
is likely to be deficient if used on an object at a great
distance, and *vice versa.* If it produces a perfect image on
a small plate, it almost certainly fails to do so on a large
plate. And if it covers a large plate satisfactorily, it may
be deficient if used for a very small image. The use of a
small aperture and the sacrifice of rapidity is the only
method of making a lens produce good definition in cases for
which it is not expressly designed; and, conversely, great

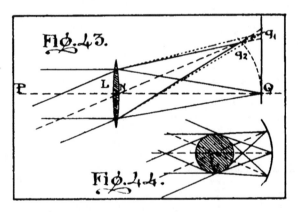

extra rapidity can only be gained by sacrificing definition
to a certain extent.

51. CURVATURE OF THE FIELD.—In explaining the different
forms of aberration, it is desirable for the sake of clearness
to assume that one form only is present at one time. This
can seldom be the case with any of the aberrations, as each
of them is usually complicated by the presence of others;
but, assuming simple curvature of the field (see Sec. 21)
to be alone present, then the foci of the direct and
various oblique pencils will lie, not in one plane, but on
a curved surface, which may be considered to be approximately spherical in curvature. With a simple positive lens
the image surface is concave to the lens, but over correction

may render it convex, or introduce negative curvature of the field.

To produce a plane image of an infinitely distant plane object the oblique pencils should be of greater focal length than a direct pencil, compare Nq_1 with NQ in fig. 43 ; but with an uncorrected positive lens their focal length is too short, as shown at Nq_2, and at q_1 a blur is produced upon the screen, as shown by broken lines. The oblique pencils being too convergent, can be corrected by a negative compensating lens, which, if compensation is alone relied upon (a somewhat unusual condition), must be a fairly powerful lens and be separated to a certain extent from the positive lens. Such a combination will give a flat field only for an object at a particular distance. The correction is likely to be insufficient for a more distant object and excessive for a near one.*

If a lens possesses spherical aberration the curvature of the field is affected very considerably by the position of the diaphragm, but in the complete absence of spherical aberration the diaphragm has no effect upon curvature, though, as with all other aberration, a small aperture will produce better definition. The effect of the diaphragm is of great importance, but it must be considered later.

In an uncorrected lens the actual curvature of the field varies with the curvatures, materials, thicknesses, and separations of the component lenses ; and also with the position of the diaphragm and distance of object. If, however, we consider only a simple single lens without a diaphragm, we may say that the radius of curvature of the field, when the incident light is parallel, is usually between one quarter and one half the focal length of the lens, while in exceptional cases it may be greater than half the focal length ; for example, in the case of a spherical lens, the radius of the field must be equal to the focal length (see fig. 44).

It may be said that a perfectly plane field is hardly to be attained. At the best we must expect the field to have either a slight curvature of positive or negative nature,

---

* This applies more or less accurately in the case of all the aberrations. Each can, however, be approximately corrected for any distance, but not all simultaneously.

or a reflex curvature that does not depart very far from the plane.

52. SPHERICAL ABERRATION IN DIRECT PENCILS.—Spherical aberration has been defined as want of sphericity in the wavefront of an emergent pencil. A longitudinal central section of a direct pencil then intersects the wavefront in a curve of a symmetrical, but non-circular form.

Suppose in figs. 45 and 46 *ac* to be the trace of a spherical wavefront of a perfect direct pencil, and *dbe*

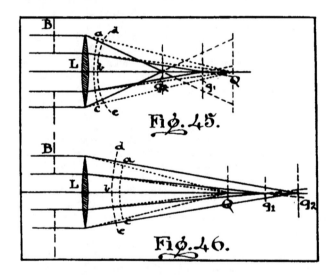

Fig. 45.

Fig. 46.

to be that of the non-spherical real front. All rays normal to *ac* would come to one focus at *Q*, but normals to *dbe* will come to different foci q_1, q_2, etc., and *Q* will be the focus only for infinitely close central rays; marginal rays coming to either a nearer focus, as in fig. 45, or to a more distant one as in fig. 46. The first figure illustrates the positive spherical aberration characteristic of un-corrected positive lenses; the marginal rays are too convergent, a defect that can be compensated by a negative lens. Over compensation will then render marginal rays insufficiently convergent, and produce the negative form of aberration shown in fig. 46.

It will be noticed that the foci of corresponding pairs of rays are displaced longitudinally along the axis of the pencil. This particular form of aberration may therefore be distinguished as longitudinal spherical aberration, and as all foci lie between Q and q_2, the distance Qq_2 may be taken as a measure of the aberration.

In fig. 47 is shown on a larger scale the distribution of the light between the extreme foci Q and q_2. Negative aberration being precisely the opposite of positive aberration, these foci may be considered to belong to a

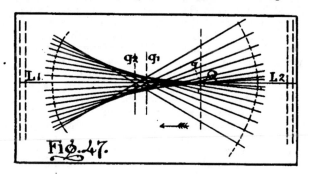

Fig. 47.

pencil emergent either from a lens L_1 with positive aberration, or from L_2 with negative aberration. The intersections of consecutive rays cause the illumination to be more intense along the axis and the outside of the pencil, and there is the greatest accumulation of light in the smallest compass, and therefore the brightest focus, at a point q, very near Q. This may be considered to be the best attainable focus, but it is surrounded by a considerable amount of blur of less intensity. If we move the focussing-screen in the direction of the arrow the blur diminishes, while the central spot increases and becomes less bright, until at q_1 * the blur has disappeared and we have a ring of light surrounding a central bright spot, or disc of light.

---

* This point does not agree with q_1 in figs. 45 and 46.

Still farther towards q_2 the centre spot disappears and beyond q_2 we have the appearance of a ring of light surrounding a comparatively dark centre. The points of best focus q, and of mean focus q_1, are easily distinguished on the screen, and if the mean focus is between the best focus and the lens the aberration is positive, while if the mean focus is farther from the lens than the best focus the aberration is negative. This affords a good means of testing aberration, and so also does the appearance of the dark centre beyond q_2.

Referring again to figs. 45 and 46, it will be evident that by placing a diaphragm at B the outer rays of the pencils are eliminated and the longitudinal aberration is reduced in extent to Qq_1. The size of the mean focus and of the blur around the best focus are reduced also, and there is an alteration in the distribution of the light shown in fig. 47; the points q_1 and q both moving towards Q. Therefore, if we take the best focus q as the principal focus of the lens, the focal length of the lens apparently increases with the small aperture if the aberration is positive, and diminishes if the aberration is negative. With any lens in which the diaphragm is mainly relied on for the purpose of correcting spherical aberration, and especially with single combinations, the best focus is thus liable to shift with variations in the size of the aperture; hence, whenever possible, it is desirable to focus with the working stop that is to be used for exposure.

The amount of spherical aberration possessed by a single lens depends to a great extent on the form of the lens, a minimum amount being present in the case of a crossed lens in which the surface nearest the principal focus has a curvature of one-sixth that of the other surface.

With all forms of lenses the aberration in direct pencils is greatest when the side of greatest curvature is nearest to the image. Hence with a positive meniscus there is less spherical aberration when the concave side is towards the image; but this position is disadvantageous as regards oblique pencils, and the opposite position, concave towards the object, has perforce to be adopted in spite of the large amount of spherical aberration that is then introduced.

Form has also to be considered in the compensating lens, and as form is restricted if the lenses are cemented, greater control is obtained by keeping them separate. If too far apart the aberration is under corrected, and if too near it is over corrected. With cemented lenses the contact surface must be negative, and one such surface alone will not compensate more than a moderate amount of spherical aberration. If then the combination as a whole is of the meniscus form, and is used with the concave side to the object, the one contact surface will fail to completely compensate the aberration. If, however, a small aperture is used to cut out the more violently aberrated outer rays the small central pencil may be fairly well compensated. In telescopic objectives more complete compensation is possible because the meniscus form of lens can be reversed. The slight amount of positive aberration possessed by a crossed lens can be corrected by one contact surface.

53. SPHERICAL ABERRATION IN OBLIQUE PENCILS.—With an oblique pencil longitudinal sections taken through the central ray are dissimilar, varying according to the inclination of the section. To take the simplest possible case, assume that the lens is infinitely thin so that all oblique axial rays are straight, and also central to their respective pencils. The lens being circular, a pencil passing obliquely through it is elliptical in transverse section, and a longitudinal section of the pencil taken through the shortest diameter of the ellipse will lie in one plane with the principal axis of the lens. Such a section is designated as a section in primary plane. Thus, when we show on a diagram a section of both a direct and an oblique pencil, the latter must be shown in primary plane, which is the plane of the paper on which the diagram is drawn.

A section of the oblique pencil made in a plane at right angles to the primary plane and taken through the longest diameter of the ellipse is called a section in secondary plane. In the simple case we have assumed this section would pass through the axis of the oblique pencil, but if the axial ray was not the central ray, the section might be some way from the axis. Between these two sections we might take any number of others at varying degrees of inclination from the primary plane, but, as sections in

primary and secondary plane differ the most it is sufficient
to consider them only.

Assuming an oblique emergent pencil to be free from
spherical aberration, its wavefront is spherical, and sections
of the wavefront in primary and secondary planes are both
circular and concentric to the same centre or focus. If
the wavefront is non-spherical varying conditions may exist.
1st. The sections may be non-circular, but each of symmetrical curvature, in which case there is longitudinal
spherical aberration as already described. *2nd.* The primary
section of the wavefront may be not only non-circular but
also unsymmetrical in form, in which case we have the effect
of coma. A longitudinal section in secondary plane is
always symmetrical. *3rd.* Both sections may be circular,
or approximately so, but be concentric to different centres
or foci, in which case the effect of astigmatism is produced.

If the aberration is longitudinal only, the effect is similar
to that in direct pencils; but if a diaphragm is used to
correct it, the curvature of the field is considerably affected
by varying the position of the diaphragm. Suppose, for
example, we have a simple lens *L*, producing either positive
longitudinal spherical aberration as shown in primary
plane in fig. 48, or negative similar aberration as in
fig. 49. If the diaphragm is placed at the crossing-point
C, its effect is similar to that of a diaphragm in the case
of a direct pencil. The focal length of the oblique pencil
is slightly altered by variations in the size of the aperture,
and therefore the curvature of field is very slightly
affected; but if the stop be placed at *A*, away from the
crossing-point, so as to eliminate all rays in primary plane
excepting such as come to foci at *q*, a very considerable
effect is produced upon curvature. With positive aberration, as in fig. 48, the emergent pencil is shortened and
curvature of the field increased; and with negative aberration, as in fig. 49, the field is flattened (assuming that
curvature already exists) or even rendered convex, the
focus *q* being thrown farther from the lens. Thus the
existence of negative aberration assists in the attainment
of a flat field so far as the primary plane of the oblique
pencil is concerned. The farther the stop is from the
crossing-point the greater is its effect.

Incidentally it may be noted that the foci q, q, are thrown off the axial ray, hence the image is geometrically inaccurate, or distorted.

Variations in the position of the stop similarly affect the focus of the oblique pencil in secondary plane, but in a somewhat different manner and to a different extent. There is a different secondary plane with its own focus for every position of the stop, and the farther the stop is from the lens the farther is the secondary plane from

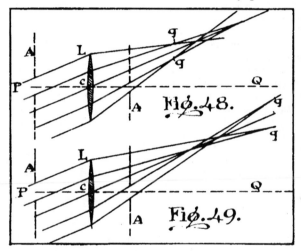

Fig. 48.

Fig. 49.

the axial ray of the oblique pencil. The focal length is shortened if the aberration is positive, and lengthened if negative; but the effect of the stop on the focal length in secondary plane is only one-third the amount of its effect in primary plane.*

* It may be observed that the effects of a diaphragm may be produced, though no actual diaphragm is present. Some portion of the lens mount may cut off parts of oblique pencils and act as a partial diaphragm; or, one lens of a doublet may act as a diaphragm to the other. An alteration in the length of the mount, or in the separation of the lenses, then has a similar effect to that produced by a similar alteration in the distance between a single lens and its stop.

It should be noted that if the stop is at C, in figs. 48 and 49, the secondary plane passes through the straight oblique axial ray; but if the stop is at A, the secondary plane passes through the central ray of the narrow pencil transmitted by the stop, and is not straight but bent at the lens.

As the effect of the stop differs in primary and secondary plane, the two planes may have different foci, or the pencil may be astigmatic. This illustrates the fact that astigmatism is only a particular phase of spherical aberration, and also that it may be produced by a misplacement of the stop under certain conditions. In a simple lens, however, it exists independently of the stop which may be employed to cure it.

54. COMA.—In fig. 50 assume we have a lens L, the principal axis of which is represented by PQ. The axis of an oblique pencil is represented by pqr, and the section of this pencil is shown in primary plane. In the absence of spherical aberration, the emergent plane pencil has a circular wavefront ac, and comes to a focus at q. If, however, coma exists, the section of the wavefront is both non-circular and non-symmetrical, being, with the form of lens shown, more sharply curved below the axis than above it, as shown at dbe, with the result that corresponding opposite pairs of rays come to foci q_1, q_2, etc., above the axis, and this produces a blur on one side of the true focus-point q in a direction away from the principal axis PQ. Assuming a screen to be placed at q, then, instead of an image point, we shall have a one-sided blur; while, if we assume curvature of the field to exist, and the screen to be at Q, the additional blur, due to the curvature, will not be circular, as it would be in the absence of coma, but of an irregular pear shape; this appearance being a test for coma.

If this figure is compared with figs. 48 and 49, it will be noticed that while those two show longitudinal displacement of the foci of corresponding pairs of rays, fig. 50 shows lateral displacement of similar foci. Coma may therefore be described as due to lateral spherical aberration.

Fig. 50 illustrates outward coma, but if the lens is reversed, as in fig. 51, the foci q_1, q_2, etc., are laterally displaced towards the principal axis, and produce the reversed effect of inward coma. If two such lenses are combined in reversed positions, as in the ordinary doublet, the inward coma of one is neutralised by the outward coma of the other, and lateral aberration is compensated, this being an example of positive compensation. Further, as opposite forms of the aberration are given by simply reversing the

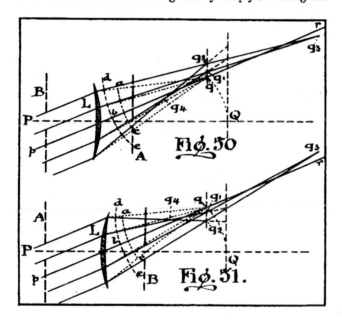

curvatures of the lens, it is possible, as pointed out by Mr. Dennis Taylor, to select an intermediate form of lens that shall be free from coma. This will be a crossed lens of approximately the same form as that which possesses a minimum amount of longitudinal spherical aberration (see Sec. 52).

With single lenses, or combinations of the meniscus form, it is usual to rely on the diaphragm to eliminate the majority of the rays that produce the coma. Thus if we place a diaphragm at B (figs. 50 and 51) only a portion of the large pencil is allowed to pass, and this comes to a focus at q_2. In connection with this effect of the diaphragm, there are several matters to notice.

First, the focus q_3 is farther from the lens than the other foci q, q_1, and q_2, and by carefully adjusting the position of the diaphragm we can arrange matters so that q_3 comes exactly on the screen passing through Q, and so produces a flat field image. The farther the diaphragm is from the lens the farther is q_3, hence, as in the diagram, q_3 is beyond the screen and the field is over corrected, B is too far from the lens. If the diaphragm were on the other side of the lens at A, curvature would be increased, not diminished (see foci q_4).

Second, it will be noticed that q_3 is below the axis in fig. 50 and above it in 51, being on the opposite side to the coma in each case. This lateral displacement of the foci off the axis renders the image geometrically incorrect, or distorts it in a direction opposite to that of the coma. It is thus apparent that the effect of the stop with coma is very similar to its effect with longitudinal aberration. If positive longitudinal aberration exists simultaneously with coma, the effect of the stop with the one aberration may be counteracted by its effect with the other, and the lens may be considered to be free from diaphragm corrections so far as they affect curvature. This is taken advantage of in the Cooke lens, in which compensation is alone relied upon to cure curvature.

55. ASTIGMATISM.—The curvatures of the wavefront in primary and secondary plane may both be circular, but they may not have a common centre, in which case each plane has a different focus. This produces the effect known as astigmatism, which is better described as astigmatic spherical aberration. As before, we need consider only the extreme sections in primary and secondary plane.

The existence of astigmatism is shown by the blurring of the image in two particular opposite directions which vary with the position of the screen. If the screen is at the focus of the primary plane the image of a point is blurred in secondary plane and becomes a line. Conversely if the screen is at the secondary focus, the image is blurred in primary plane. At intermediate positions, between the primary and secondary foci, the image is out of focus in both planes, and at one point it will be blurred equally in both directions, so that the image of a point becomes approximately a disc; this, being the nearest approach to a regular point that can be attained, may be called the mean focus.* Thus there are three astigmatic foci to the oblique pencil, the primary, mean, and secondary foci, and while the best image of a point is to be obtained at the mean focus, the best image of a line lying in primary plane

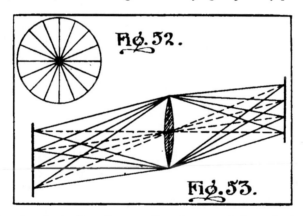

is to be obtained at the secondary focus, and that of a line in secondary plane at the primary focus.

Suppose that in the object there are a series of lines all radiating from a point on the principal axis of the lens, as in fig. 52. As a line may be considered to consist of an infinite number of points, the image of one of these lines will be formed by an infinite series of oblique pencils, a few of which are shown in fig. 53, all in primary plane. As the object line itself is in primary plane a blur in primary

* Some writers state erroneously that the mean astigmatic image of a point is a cross. If a lens has a circular aperture the primary and secondary foci are very attenuated ellipses (practically lines) at right angles to one another, and it is not possible for a cross to be formed between these two foci.

plane of each image point will be of no consequence; it will simply overlap the other points and slightly lengthen the line; hence, if the light pencils are astigmatic, the best image of a radial line will be produced at their secondary foci, at which any blur is in a primary direction. If, however, in addition to the radial lines, we have a circle, as shown in fig. 52, the image of that circle, being blurred radially, will be quite out of focus. If now the screen is moved to the primary focus of the oblique pencils, any point in the circle will be blurred in secondary plane, or at right angles, or tangential, to the radii; hence the

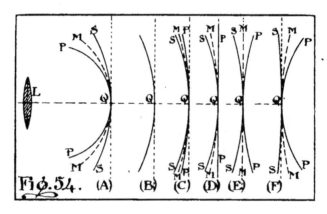

Fig. 54. (A) (B) (C) (D) (E) (F)

circle will be in focus while the radii, being blurred tangentially, will be out of focus. We cannot in any way bring both the circle and the radii into focus together, which fact is a proof of the existence of astigmatism. An object such as that shown in fig. 52 is a very convenient test object for this aberration. On account of these radial and tangential effects, the primary focus is often called the tangent focus, and the secondary focus the radial focus. They are also sometimes respectively distinguished as the meridional and sagittal foci.

The separation of the astigmatic foci increases with the obliquity of the pencils (as do all other aberrations to which oblique pencils are subject), and as there are three foci to every pencil there are also three focal fields—the primary, mean, and secondary ; two of which, at least, must be curved fields. With a simple positive lens all three fields are curved, see *P*, *M*, and *S* in fig. 54A, the primary field being of greater curvature or shorter radius than the others. The three fields coincide only at the direct focus *Q*, at which there is no astigmatism. This is an illustration of positive astigmatism, and the amount of the astigmatism may be represented by the ratio of the curvatures of the primary and secondary fields.

It is apparent that to cure astigmatism, or to render the lens anastigmatic, all three fields must be brought together ; and to cure curvature the one field produced must be flat. If we attempt to flatten the fields by any means not affecting the material or the curvatures of the lens (see Sec. 51), the primary field is affected just three times as much as the secondary field; hence, if the primary field has originally three times the curvature of the secondary field, the correction of curvature involves that of astigmatism, the two fields coinciding at the moment when both are flat. This cannot, however, be accomplished with ordinary single lenses, for with such the primary field has only about twice the curvature of the secondary field, and therefore the two come together before either of them is flat, and they produce one curved non-astigmatic field, as shown in fig. 54B. If the flattening process is carried further the primary field passes the secondary field and the astigmatism is over corrected and becomes negative, as shown in 54C to F. The extent to which this over correction may be carried is considerable. In 54C slight negative astigmatism has been introduced, but the average curvature is less than in 54B. In 54D the primary field is flat, but negative astigmatism has increased. In 54E, the mean field is flat, while the primary and secondary field are of opposite curvatures. In 54F the secondary field is approximately flat, while the mean and primary fields have negative curvatures. Figs. 52D, E, F, may be taken to represent the average state of correction of "flat field" astigmatic lenses of the ordinary types, E being perhaps the most useful degree of correction. Fig. 52C may represent a "round field" lens, the curvature of the anastigmatic field in 52B being too great to render such a type of lens of much utility.

To render all three fields flat the materials and surfaces of the lens must be so adjusted as to increase the initial astigmatism to the required ratio of 3—1. This can be accomplished by combining a negative and positive lens so that the contact surface is positive; but this condition is directly opposite to that essential to the correction of longitudinal spherical aberration, which requires the contact surface to be negative. Thus, with two cemented lenses, the preliminary increase of astigmatism necessary to its correction simultaneously with curvature of field involves an increase of longitudinal aberration, while the compensation of the latter reduces astigmatism to such an extent as to render it impossible to simultaneously correct it and secure a flat field.

The difficulty can be got over by employing extra surfaces. Thus by combining four lenses, so arranged that the contact surface in one pair is negative and in the other pair positive, the required condition for longitudinal correction can then be fulfilled in the first pair, and that for astigmatism and curvature in the second; while any residue of aberration of a positive nature in one combination can be neutralised by an excess of negative aberration in the other. This method is employed in certain of the Zeiss lenses. Such a doublet is non-separable, as the removal of either combination disturbs the correction of the whole.

The arrangement may be varied by employing one lens in place of the two interior ones. That is, by combining three lenses with two contact surfaces, one negative and one positive. A corrected single combination can be formed in this way, and two such combinations may form a separable doublet, such as the Goerz double anastigmat.

The system may be further varied by combining two separated lenses so that of the adjacent surfaces one may be positive and the other negative. We then practically have a lens of air enclosed between two of glass. This method is also employed in the Goerz lenses. Further; two such combinations may be combined to form a doublet, and if the two interior negative lenses are coalesced into one, we have a triplet very similar to the Cooke lens. The one central negative lens then compensates the aberrations of the two other positive lenses. The Cooke lens is specially distinguished by the employment of single lenses free from diaphragm corrections (see Sec. 54), and of only one compensating lens to simultaneously correct the three primary aberrations.

There are many possible modifications, but the systems mentioned sufficiently illustrate the methods employed, as a general rule, in lenses that are corrected for astigmatic and longitudinal aberration, and for curvature; but there are a few exceptional methods. As, for example, we may ignore the compensation of longitudinal spherical aberration and rely upon the stop to eliminate it as far as possible. This renders the lens slow and Ross' Concentric is a type of such a slow anastigmatic flat-field lens. It may be mentioned that this lens owes its name to the fact that in each of its two combinations the outer lens surfaces are approximately concentric, so that the lenses are of approximately equal thickness in all parts. This is a condition that is very closely observed in all combinations that produce primary and secondary fields with curvatures in the ratio of 3 to 1.

56. EXPLANATORY NOTES.—It should be understood that the terms coma and astigmatism are only descriptive of secondary effects produced by spherical aberration in oblique pencils. Similar effects might be due to other quite different causes. For example, if there is any defect in the curvatures of the lens surfaces, either coma or astigmatism will appear in direct pencils as well as in oblique ones. The appearance of these effects only in oblique pencils indicates that spherical aberration exists. Some photographic writers apply the term spherical aberration only to the longitudinal displacement of the foci of pencils of different diameter, and apparently look upon astigmatism as a separate aberration altogether, and this erroneous distinction has led to a good deal of confusion. It is worthy of note that Glazebrook in his "Physical Optics" avoids the use of any distinctive terms, describing all the effects of spherical aberration under the simple heading of aberration. If spherical aberration is considered to be

6

divided into three varieties; longitudinal, lateral, and astigmatic spherical aberration,—respectively distinguished by symmetrical, non-symmetrical, or linear blurs—the subject is much simplified.

57. CHROMATIC ABERRATION.—This has been defined as the separation of a wavefront of compound light into separate wavefronts of light of different colours, or, as the dispersion of a ray of compound light into rays of different colours, which converge on different foci.

Chromatic aberration is cured by the employment of compensating lenses. With a positive lens violet rays are rendered too strongly convergent as compared with, say, the yellow; but with a negative lens they are too strongly divergent, hence one lens will compensate the other.

The peculiar difficulty of chromatic correction is the simultaneous correction of more than two colours, and as the photographic plate is sensitive to a considerable range of colours, correction for two only is generally insufficient. If the dispersive powers of various materials for different pairs of rays were always in the same proportion, the correction of any two rays would involve that of the others. This not being the case, it is generally necessary to employ additional lenses or surfaces to eliminate all such secondary or residual aberration as may be of importance.

With modern varieties of glass dispersive power and refractive power do not necessarily vary together, and it is possible for a contact surface between two lenses to produce positive refraction and negative dispersion; that is to say, the material of one lens may be of higher refractive power but of lower dispersive power than the other. Thus chromatic aberration, astigmatism, and curvature may be simultaneously corrected. Before the invention of Jena glass, however, dispersive and refractive power always varied together; hence it was only possible to simultaneously correct longitudinal spherical aberration and chromatic aberration. The chromatic correction being of great importance, astigmatic flat field lenses could not be produced. The general principles of their construction were understood, but the necessary material was not available.

A pair of lenses arranged to correct spherical and chromatic aberration is called a "normal" or "old" achromat,

A pair arranged for the corrections of astigmatism,
curvature, and chromatic aberration as an "abnormal" or
"new" achromat. Thus, the Concentric is formed of two
abnormal achromats. The ordinary "rectilinear" of two
normal achromats. The Zeiss, referred to in Sec. 55, of
one normal and one abnormal achromat.

The diaphragm has no curative effect upon chromatic
aberration, excepting so far as the aperture can be reduced
to diminish the diameter of the blur. The presence of
chromatic aberration is indicated by the colouration of the
margin of the blur around the focus, but the best test is
to expose a plate on a series of numbered cards at various
distances from the lens, focussing carefully on one particular
number. If that number is the best defined in the developed
image the lens is achromatic, but if a nearer number is
better defined, positive aberration exists, or if a farther
number, then there is negative aberration.

58. DIAPHRAGM DISTORTION.—It has been incidentally
explained (Secs. 53 and 54) that the use of a diaphragm
to flatten the field of oblique pencils possessing either
longitudinal spherical aberration or coma throws the image
of a point off the oblique axial ray and renders the image
geometrically incorrect. The distortion thus produced
may be either inward (all oblique pencils coming to foci
too near the principal axis) or outward (the foci being too
far from the principal axis). The former variety is produced
with single lenses of the usual landscape type with the
diaphragm on the object side of the lens; the latter is
produced if the lens is reversed so that the diaphragm is
between the lens and image.

The amount of the distortion increases with the obliquity
of the pencils. Thus, if the object happens to be a series
of concentric equidistant circles, as shown by dotted lines
in fig. 55, inward distortion will produce a contracted
image, as shown by full lines in *A*, and outward distortion
an expanded image, as shown in *B*. If the distortion is
very appreciable, a square object, such as shown in fig. 56A
will not only be contracted, but its diagonals *aa* will suffer
greater contraction than its diameters *bb*, so that the sides
will become curved as in *B*. This is known as barrel distortion. Similarly if the square suffers expansion from outward

distortion it will take the form shown at *C*, which is known as cushion distortion. All lines that pass through the principal axis of the lens remain straight while all others become curved, on which account diaphragm distortion is often termed curvilinear distortion, and a lens free from distortion is called rectilinear.* It appears, however, to be possible for a certain amount of distortion to be present without the production of any marked curvilinear effects. The best test for diaphragm distortion is therefore the comparison of proportions. For example, if we take an equally divided object, and the lens throws an equally

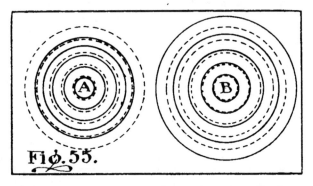

Fig. 55.

divided image on a screen parallel to the object, diaphragm distortion must be absent.

Speaking generally, distortion is diminished by placing the diaphragm at or near the crossing-point of the lens. This condition cannot be fulfilled with a single meniscus lens, as the crossing-point is on the convex side of the lens and the diaphragm must be on the concave side to diminish curvature of the field (figs. 50 and 51). In a doublet with the crossing-point between the lenses the diaphragm can be placed in the required position, but with a doublet of the periscopic form it cannot. In the telephotographic lens, which is essentially a combination of a positive and

---

* It may also be correctly described as "Orthoscopic." The particular lens (now out of date) known by this title was, however, thus christened in error, for it eventually proved to be non-rectilinear.

a negative system, distortion may be obviated by making each lens itself rectilinear. Practically each lens has a diaphragm at its own crossing-point, hence the whole is free from distortion.

It should be noted that combinations of lenses may show distortion even though no actual diaphragm is present. This may be due to the lens mount limiting the aperture and serving as a diaphragm, or to each lens serving as a diaphragm to the other (see footnote to Sec. 53), but in the absence of anything capable of serving as a diaphragm, any apparent distortion is really an effect of coma, which, from its nature, not only blurs but also distorts the image. In

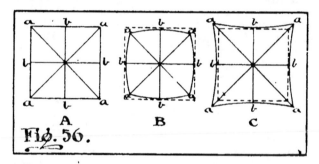

A B C

Fig. 56.

such a case, outward coma is accompanied by inward distortion and *vice versa.* This effect of coma must be carefully distinguished from diaphragm distortion.

If a lens is perfectly free from spherical aberration in oblique pencils no distortion is produced by any position of the diaphragm, and the less the part played by the diaphragm in correcting the aberrations the less is the distortion. If spherical aberration is well compensated, as it is in a high class single lens, we may expect less distortion than with a cheap achromatic single lens, even though the diaphragm is equally far removed from the crossing-point.

It should be noted that in subjects possessing no straight lines, diaphragm curvilinear distortion may have no disadvantage; on the contrary, inward or barrel distortion has the advantage of simulating the proportions of the object as they appear to the eye in visual perspective. The image is not in plane perspective, but in a sort of pseudo-spherical perspective, and is less likely to convey a false impression of distance and comparative size. On the other hand, the presence of distortion renders a photograph quite valueless as a record from which dimensions and distances are to be measured.

59. EFFECT OF ABERRATION ON THE ACTION OF LENSES.— When studying the theoretical action of a lens in forming the image, it was assumed that the lens was perfectly free from all forms of aberration. If spherical aberration is present the cardinal points and image field of a lens are rendered more or less variable. The nodes and foci are liable to shift for pencils of different widths, or of different obliquity, or for objects at varying distances. The focal length may vary with different-sized apertures, and the form of the image field may vary with the aperture and distance of objects.

With chromatic aberration the nodes, foci, focal length, and field will all vary for light pencils of different wavelengths, or for objects of different colours.

Chromatic aberration should be practically absent in a lens of moderately good quality, but a slight amount of spherical aberration is likely to remain, and also there is very probably a certain amount of variable curvature of the field for objects at varying distances.

The results of calculations with regard to foci, etc., based on the assumption that the lens acts with theoretical accuracy are likely to be slightly upset by these residual aberrations. For example, it is not safe to rely solely on calculated conjugate distances when adjusting an enlarging camera ; a visual test is necessary.

60. FLARE.—This is not an aberration of the true image, but an effect due to the production of sundry false images by the agency of reflection.

Flare may be due solely to reflections from the lens surfaces, or partly to reflections from the lens mount ; in the former case the effect may be distinguished as optical flare, in the latter as mechanical flare. Mechanical flare leads to a local or general degradation of the image

by reflected diffused light; optical flare produces similar
effects by the agency of numerous false images, which,
being non-coincident with the true image, confuse it to a
certain extent.   There is no perfect cure for flare, as no
lens can be absolutely free from it.   Mechanical flare can
be diminished by careful design and construction; and by
adjustment of surfaces, separations, and diaphragm, false
images of optical flare may be thrown into positions where
their effect is least detrimental.

The false images due to optical flare may be divided into
two classes—the secondary inverted images, formed by
single lenses, and tertiary erect images, formed by doublet
combinations.

In the case of a single meniscus lens, concave side to

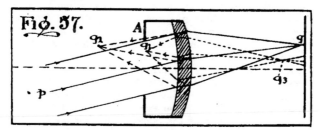

the object, an oblique pencil Pq (fig. 57) produces three
false images of the object p, in addition to the one true
image q.   Two of these images (q_1 and q_2) are in front of
the lens, and one (q_3) behind it, all three being inverted
in the same way as the true image.   The image q_2 is caused
by reflection alone from the front surface of the lens, which
acts as a concave mirror.   The image q_1 by reflection from
the back surface of the lens, which acts also as a concave
mirror; in this case all rays that reach q_1 twice suffer
refraction at the front surface.   The third image (q_3) is
formed by rays that suffer refraction at the first surface,
reflection at the second, a second reflection at the first
(which serves as a convex mirror) and then refraction
at the second surface.

All three false images can be seen upon screens placed
at the respective foci if the light from p is sufficiently

intense, but if a diaphragm is placed at A in front of the lens the pencils forming q_1 and q_2 are likely to be obstructed, and the back of the diaphragm being illuminated by them, may produce a certain amount of mechanical flare. The pencil forming q_3 is not thus obstructed by the diaphragm, but it should be noted that if the aperture is large q_3 will lie within the pencil forming q, while a small aperture will so reduce the width of the pencil as to leave q_3 outside it, and therefore more distinct. All three false foci are on the same side of the principal axis as the true image (q).

If q_3 is close to the plate on which the true image is received, an out-of-focus false image is apparent on the plate between the true image and the principal axis; but if q_3 is close to the lens, this out-of-focus image is so expanded as to produce simply a general effect of fog, and the detrimental effect of the false focus is minimised. The position of q_3 depends on the surfaces and thickness of the lens, and the distance of the diaphragm A from the lens. If the distance of the diaphragm is increased, q_3 moves towards the lens; if A is brought close to the lens, q_3 comes nearer the plate. If we have a number of oblique pencils, each one has a false focus similar to q_3, and the greater the obliquity of the pencils the farther are the false foci from the principal axis; but in no case does the false focus move very far from the axis, hence it follows that if these foci are near the plate they produce an accumulated effect in the centre of it, with the result that an over-exposed blurred patch, commonly called a flare-spot, appears. If the false foci are near the lens the flare-spot is so expanded as to produce uniform slight fog over the whole image. By shifting the diaphragm the flare-spot may be thus distributed and the defect practically, though not actually, cured.

With a rectilinear doublet, (see fig. 58) similar reflected secondary images are produced by each of the lenses, but the reflections for which the front lens is alone responsible are of little importance. Its front surface being convex light reflected from it is dispersed. From its back surface a false front focus (q_6), is produced; but all this light is lost. The back false focus corresponding to q_3 in fig. 64

is also of no account, as it is not likely to be anywhere near the plate. As regards the back lens the conditions are similar to those in fig. 57. There is a back false focus (q_3) which may be productive of flare-spot, and also front false foci corresponding to q_1 and q_2. The nearer of these two foci (q_1), is not likely to produce any effect, but the reflected pencil forming the farther one (q_2), will be reflected from the back surface of the front lens, producing a false tertiary focus between the back lens and the plate, and on the opposite side of the principal axis to the true focus q. This tertiary focus in the only one of consequence ; it is shown at q_4. Any image formed by such a focus is erect, not inverted.

The effect of this tertiary focus depends again on its

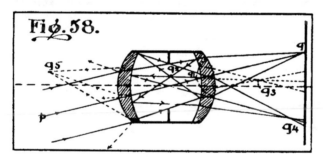

Fig. 58.

distance from the plate, and the distance is affected very considerably by the separation of the lenses. At a certain distance apart the tertiary erect image is sharply defined on the screen ; a very slight alteration in either direction will, however, throw it right out of focus and render it negligible.

Tertiary flare is not in any way responsible for flare-spot, which, as already described, is purely an effect of secondary flare. Flare-spot is a very much out-of-focus small scale inverted image of the whole view situated in the centre of the true image, and the spot will resolve itself into a fairly well defined image if the camera is racked in sufficiently. Tertiary flare, on the other hand, is a false image on much the same scale as the true image, but reversed in every particular. If we focus a gas flame near one side of the plate a corresponding erect image of the gas flame will appear on the opposite side of the plate. This is tertiary flare, and it is detrimental if both images are visible at the same time, but of little moment if we have to throw the true image out of focus to render the tertiary image apparent. If we rack in quite close to the lens secondary flare will appear in the form of a small inverted image of the flame between the true image and the centre of the plate. If there is no out-of-focus trace of this image when the true image is in focus there is not likely to be any flare spot. In this way we can readily test whether flare of an objectionable nature is present. If we photograph a landscape with a very brilliant sky, flare spot will appear in the centre of the plate if secondary flare is present in a disadvantageous form, and the foreground may be covered and degraded by a reversed, out-of-focus image of the sky if tertiary flare is a serious defect; this can, however, only be the case with doublet lenses, while flare-spot may appear with any form of lens.

The various secondary and tertiary foci that have been described as of little moment may contribute in some degree to mechanical flare, and to the production of general fog. Probably the whole of the interior metal work of the lens is illuminated directly or indirectly during exposure, and a good deal of the light reflected or dispersed from the metal work may reach the plate. Further, the plate itself, if brightly illuminated in any part, reflects light, and may serve as a source of light that may be reflected from the mount or the lenses on to another portion of the plate. So far as the mount is concerned, careful design and dead-black will minimise reflections. It is obvious that by combining a number of lenses the number of reflective surfaces is increased, and there is therefore greater likelihood of flare appearing in some form. By cementing the lenses together the reflective surfaces are reduced in number (see Sec. 12) and so also are the false foci. For example, suppose we have a combination of three lenses. If the three are separated there are six refractive and reflective surfaces; if cemented, there are four refractive and only two reflective surfaces. There is then a gain both in rapidity (less light being lost) and freedom from flare. But such gain may be counter-balanced by inefficient correction of the refractive aberrations, owing to the reduced number of refractive surfaces; and inefficient correction may require a reduction of aperture and a loss of rapidity greatly in excess of the gain due to minimised reflections. It may be noticed that in modern lenses there is a tendency to use separated rather than cemented lenses, and as a result there is a considerable number of reflective surfaces. The absence of obvious flare with such lenses must therefore be put down to the careful adjustment of separations, etc.

Many other false foci beyond those that have been mentioned are produced in a doublet lens, but they are generally so faint as to be of no moment.

CHAPTER VI.

SCALE, INTENSITY AND ILLUMINATION.

61. SCALE OF IMAGE —It has already been explained that the ratio of the linear dimensions of the image to those of the object is the ratio of the focal distance of the image to that of the object; or that, as stated in formula 1 (Sec. 19),

$$R = \frac{v}{u}$$

This general formula covers all cases, but there are special cases to consider.

If we compare the value of R with different lenses focussed on the same object at a fixed distance u, it is apparent that in all cases R must vary with v, excepting only when the object is at a truly infinite distance so that the image is infinitely small and $R = o$. The size of the image is then unaffected by the value of v, which under these conditions is equal to the focal length of the lens. In other words, all lenses produce images of the same size from infinitely distant objects. This is a fact that becomes partially apparent in astronomical work, but only in the case of the farther fixed stars.* In photography

* No optical system could produce a *visible* image of an object at a truly infinite distance. The image being infinitely small, or a mathematical point, would be invisible, and could not be magnified. The distance of the known fixed stars is not truly infinite. They are near enough to produce visible images; but distant enough to prevent the size of the image from being appreciably affected by the focal length of the object glass of a telescope. This is due to the virtual parallelism of the various light pencils forming the image. The production of a visible image shows that the pencils are not truly parallel to one another, but we cannot construct a lens of sufficient focal length to enable us to take advantage of their want of parallelism, and so increase the size of the image.

we never deal with truly infinite distances, but, if we focus on such a distance by placing the plate at the principal focus of the lens, all objects beyond a certain near finite distance are also in focus; and if we assign a definite finite value to u then R varies strictly with v, which under the conditions equals f. Thus, when different lenses are working at their focal lengths, the size of the image of an object at a finite distance varies strictly with the value of f, so that an 8-in. lens will produce an image twice the size of that formed by a 4-in. lens.

If, then, we bring the object so near that we have to rack out the camera and make v greater than f, the size no longer varies with f, but simply with v. Thus, if the object is at a focal distance of 32 ins. an 8-in. lens produces an image, not twice, but $2\frac{1}{3}$ times the size of one formed by a 4-in. lens. The mistake is frequently made of assuming that in all cases the size of the image is proportional to the focal length of the lens.

We have here only considered cases in which u remains constant with different lenses. If we keep to one lens and vary the distance of the object, it is manifest that if an alteration in u involves an alteration in v to secure focus, then R varies with the value of v/u as in the formula; but if the object is at such a distance from the lens as to render an alteration of v unnecessary, then R varies inversely with u. For example, if with a 6-in. lens we reduce the distance of the object from 80 ft. to 40 ft. refocussing on the nearer distance is unnecessary, and the size of the image is simply doubled; but, if we reduced the distance from 10 to 5 ft. we should have to refocus and alter v, and as the result the larger image would be $2\frac{1}{19}$ times the size of the smaller.

62. ENLARGEMENT AND REDUCTION.—From the fundamental formula $R = v/u$ we can find one term, if the other two are known, but in the case of enlarging or reducing on a particular scale we know only R, and must find both the others for a lens of a particular focal length f, in order that we may adjust object, lens, and image at proper distances. From formula 7 in Sec. 33 we can find the extra-focal distances of image and object in terms of R and f.

The extra-focal distance of the image equals

$$x = Rf \quad \ldots \quad \ldots \quad \ldots \quad (19).$$

The extra-focal distance of the object equals

$$d = \frac{f}{R} \quad \ldots \quad \ldots \quad \ldots \quad (20).$$

By adding f to the values of x and d we can express the focal distances v and u in terms of R and f; thus

$$v = (1 + R)f \quad \ldots \quad \ldots \quad \ldots \quad (21)$$
$$u = (1 + \frac{1}{R})f \quad \ldots \quad \ldots \quad \ldots \quad (22).$$

In these formulæ we may consider the extra-focal distances x and d, and the focal distances v and u, to be represented in terms of the focal length f as a unit, which is a very convenient method of describing them. To give a few examples. If we wish to produce an enlarged image on a scale of 3 to 1 diameters, from the formulæ we can see at once that the extra-focal distance of the image is three times the focal length, and that of the object one-third the focal length, one multiplier being the reciprocal of the other; or that the focal distance of the image equals four focal lengths, and that of the object one and a third focal lengths. If then we are using a 6-in. lens the distance v equals 24 ins. and the distance u equals 8 ins.

Or to take the example given earlier in this section. If the focal distance of the object is 32 ins. and the focal length of the lens is 8 ins., u equals $4f$, hence $d = 3f$ and $x = \frac{1}{3}f$. Therefore $1/R = 3$ or $R = \frac{1}{3}$.

If the focal length is 4 ins., then $u = 8f$, $d = 7f$ and $R = \frac{1}{7}$. Hence the 8-in. lens gives an image $2\frac{1}{3}$ times as large as the 4-in. lens.

To take an example of reduction on a particular scale. Assume R to equal $\frac{1}{4}$ and f to be 8 ins. The distance v must then equal $(1 + R)\,f = 1\frac{1}{4} \times 8 = 10$ ins. The distance $u = (1 + 1/R)\,f = (1 + 4)\,8 = 40$ ins. Or, we might find u by dividing v by R, thus $10 \div \frac{1}{4} = 40$ ins.

In practice it is a very difficult matter to tentatively adjust the apparatus so as to give an image on an exact scale. The formulæ enable us to place the object, lens, and screen in approximately the correct positions, but almost always a slight extra adjustment is necessary to secure sharp focus. The focal length may not be exactly known, the nodes of the lens are probably unmarked, and there are likely to be mechanical difficulties in the way of measuring to the focussing-screen, so that an uncertain amount of error frequently appears as regards scale.

In the Appendix, Table C gives the focal distances of object and image for various values of R from $\frac{1}{25}$ up to 25, for a lens of 1-in. focal length. From these it is easy to arrive at the corresponding distances for a lens of any focal length, as we need only multiply the figures given by the focal length in inches.

63. RELATIVE INTENSITY OF ILLUMINATION.—This is a matter that directly affects exposure. The intensity of

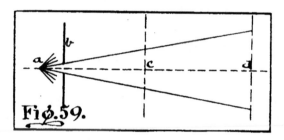

Fig. 59.

the illumination received from a constant source of light varies inversely with the square of the distance of the light. Suppose, for example, we have an infinitely small source of light a (fig. 59) from which light radiates in all directions. Placing a diaphragm b with a circular aperture near the light we can isolate one divergent pencil which will form a disc of light of a certain size on a screen placed at c, or a larger disc on a more distant screen at d. The areas of these discs vary with the squares of their diameters, and their diameters vary with the distance of the screen from the source of light a, hence the areas of the discs vary with the squares of the distances ac and ad. The total amount of light passed by the diaphragm is constant, but being distributed over a larger area on the more distant screen, the intensity of its effect is less than on the nearer screen, the intensity at corresponding portions of the discs being inversely proportional to the area of the disc, or to the distance of the screen, or as $(1/ac)^2 : (1/ad)^2$.

This "law of inverse squares" governs all problems relating to the intensity of the illumination produced by a lens, but it is important to remember that the intensity is only relative. We do not measure the actual intensity at either screen, only the comparative intensity at the two distances. Further, intensity is distinct from quantity. The two screens receive equal quantities of light, but the illumination is of different intensity.

Relative quantity may be represented by intensity multiplied by area, thus the quantity of light passed by the diaphragm is proportional to the intensity of the light at the aperture multiplied by the area of the aperture; that is, to the square of the diameter of the aperture divided by the square of its distance from the light. If we vary both diameter and distance so as to preserve a constant ratio between them, the quantity of light passed remains constant. In the case of images projected by a lens under varying conditions, if we estimate the relative quantities of light passed by the lens, and divide those quantities by the relative image areas, we arrive at the relative intensities of illumination at the various images, and from these the relative exposures required to produce a developable image. Not the actual exposures, as they require, in addition, measurement of the power of the light at its source, and of the sensitiveness or speed of the plate.

64. RELATIVE INTENSITY AND EXPOSURE.—The exposure required to produce a developable image in a camera varies inversely with the relative intensity of the light received by the plate, and this intensity can be found in the manner just described.

The amount of light transmitted by a lens from a certain luminous object point varies inversely with the square of the focal distance of the point, and directly with the area of the lens effective aperture, or, the aperture being circular, with the square of its diameter. Thus if u represents the focal distance of the point, and k is the diameter of the aperture, the light transmitted varies with the value of k^2/u^2. The total quantity transmitted by the lens from the whole of the object may be considered to be governed by the same rule if we look upon the object as consisting of a number of points. The size of the image varies, under the laws of conjugate foci, with the relative distances of image and object from the lens (see formula 1), or with the ratio of the focal distances v and u; and its area varies with the value of v^2/u^2. Dividing this relative area into the relative amount of light transmitted by the lens, we have at the image a relative intensity of illumination equal to k^2/v^2. If then we represent the diameter of the aperture in the form of a fraction of the focal distance v or as v/a,* then $k^2/v^2 = 1/a^2$, and this is the usual and most convenient method of representing the relative working intensity of the illumination of the image.

Relative exposure being inversely proportional to relative intensity, exposure is always proportional to the value of a^2.

As $k = v/a$, it follows that $a = v/k$, varying directly with the value of v and inversely with that of k. The distance v depends upon the focal length of the lens and the scale of the image, and it is important to understand clearly the effect upon intensity and exposure of any alteration in one of the three factors—size of aperture, scale of image, and focal length. Assume that we know the correct intensity and exposure for a certain object with a lens of certain power and aperture, when photographing the object on a certain scale. Under all conditions the intensity is proportionate to the value of $1/a^2$ and exposure to that of a^2, but it is not always convenient to look at the matter solely from that point of view.

Assume first that we vary the size of the aperture only; such an alteration affects a in inverse proportion—that is, if we halve the diameter of the stop we double a, and therefore increase the value of a^2 four times, hence the intensity is reduced to a quarter, and the exposure increased four times—therefore exposure varies inversely with the square of the diameter of the aperture.

Second, suppose we alter the scale of the image, using the same lens and aperture. An alteration in scale may be brought about indirectly by altering the distance

---

* This fraction is sometimes called the working "angular aperture," but I prefer the term "fractional diameter" used later on.

between lens and object and refocussing. This alters the value of v, and as a varies directly with v, $1/a^2$ varies with $1/v^2$, and therefore intensity is proportional to $1/v^2$, and exposure to v^2. Thus, if by bringing the object nearer to the lens so as produce a larger image, the value of v is increased from 7 to 10 ins. the relative exposures are in the ratio of 49 : 100, or approximately 1 : 2.

We may, however, directly alter the scale, or the value of v/u or R, and then a is still proportional to v, and v equals $(R + 1)\ F$. As F is constant v varies with $R + 1$ and the intensity varies with the value of $1 \div (R + 1)^2$, and the exposure with $(R + 1)^2$. In the example given above, assuming the focal length of the lens to be 4 ins., an extension of 7 ins. would produce an image on a reduced scale of $\frac{3}{4}$, and an extension of 10 ins. represents an enlargement of $1\frac{1}{2}$ diameters. The exposures are then in the ratio of $(\frac{3}{4} + 1)^2 : (1\frac{1}{2} + 1)^2$ or 49 : 100 as before.

Third, we may vary the focal length alone, retaining an aperture of the same diameter and producing an image of the same size. Here again a varies with v, while v equals $(R + 1)\ F$; and R being constant, v varies with F. Therefore intensity varies with the value of $1/F^2$ and exposure with F^2. For example, if we know the exposure required to produce a full size copy with a 6-in. lens and $\frac{1}{2}$ in. aperture, and want to know the exposure required to make a full size copy with an 8-in. lens and $\frac{1}{2}$ in. aperture, the exposures are in the ratio of 36 : 64 or 9 : 16.

These rules with regard to intensity and exposure for different sized images produced by one lens, or equal sized images produced by different lenses, apply especially to cases in which the object is so near the lens that the distance v and u have to be adjusted strictly in accordance with the laws of conjugate foci to secure sharp focus. When the object is anywhere beyond a certain distance from the lens, v equals f, and is not subject to variation. The size of the image then varies inversely with the distance of the object, but intensity and exposure for a certain lens remain constant with a given aperture for any distance beyond the minimum, while with different lenses of equal aperture exposure varies with the value of f^2, whether equal sized images are produced or not.

Apparent variations from these rules, in the case of varying distances, are due to the effect of the intervening atmosphere, which, being itself a luminous body, adds to the apparent luminosity of the object and renders shorter exposure desirable in the case of very distant objects.

It must be understood that however we vary scale or focal length, exposure is uniform if we preserve a constant value for a. That is, if we vary the size of the aperture so as to preserve a constant ratio between its diameter and the distance v.

Table D in the Appendix gives varying relative exposures for different degrees of enlargement or reduction with any one particular lens and aperture.

It should be observed that as with near objects an alteration in scale necessitates alterations in the distances of object and image, and such alterations with some lenses cause the size of the effective aperture of the lens to vary, or to be inconstant, the value of a may not always directly vary with that of v, and error may thus be introduced, especially when dealing with enlarged images. This error is probably in most cases a negligible quantity and may not exist at all with a doublet. The reversing of a lens with an inconstant aperture will also cause intensity to vary to a very small extent.

It will be noticed that so long as we consider relative exposures only, though so much depends on the intensity or the value of a^2, a knowledge of that value is not of much practical importance. If we vary the aperture alone we want to know simply the comparative diameters or areas of the apertures; if we vary scale we want the comparative values of either v or $r + 1$; if we vary focal length we simply want to know f. The value of $1/a^2$, which may be distinguished as the working intensity of the lens, is not actually required, excepting for the purpose of estimating the absolute exposure which serves as the basis of comparison, and to estimate which we must know not only the working intensity of the lens, but also the speed of the plate and power of the light. For the purpose of calculating absolute exposure, and for that of comparing the rapidity of different lenses, intensity must be known, but it is customary to record only the nominal intensity of the lens with each aperture. This nominal intensity is the working intensity or value of $1/a^2$ in the particular case when $v = f$, or when the lens is focussed on a distant object; but, usually, we record simply the square root of the intensity, or the value of $1/a$ which is the ratio of the diameter of the aperture to the focal length, and may therefore be styled the nominal ratio aperture.

65. MARKING APERTURES.—In describing the manner in which we arrive at the fraction $1/a^2$, representing the working intensity of the lens for a particular aperture, the actual diameter of the aperture was represented in the form of a fraction of the focal distance of the image, or as v/a. As v is a variable quantity, a (which may be styled the ratio number) also varies, but in the particular case when v is equal to f the diameter of the aperture is equal to f/a. This may be styled the fractional diameter of the aperture, to distinguish it from the absolute diameter expressed in the form of a dimension. If we divide the fractional diameter f/a by f we have $1/a$, which is the nominal ratio aperture, as described in the previous section. Squaring the nominal ratio aperture we have $1/a^2$, which is the nominal relative intensity with aperture f/a. The reciprocal of the intensity, or a^2, which is the square of the ratio number, then represents the relative exposure. Thus, the fraction f/a gives directly, or indirectly, the nominal diameter, ratio, and intensity of the aperture, and also the exposure. These are practically all the particulars necessary, for if we know the nominal intensity or exposure for any aperture, the working intensity or exposure for a different value of v is readily found by the rules previously given. Therefore, as a rule, all apertures are marked either with their fractional diameters or nominal ratio apertures. Under this system of marking, an aperture that is equal in diameter to the focal length is the unit aperture, possesses a unit intensity, and requires a unit exposure; as indicated in the following table, which shows a series of apertures decreasing in diameter in geometrical progression.

Fractional diameter	$f/_1$	$f/_2$	$f/_4$	$f/_8$	$f/_{16}$
Ratio aperture ...	1	$\frac{1}{2}$	$\frac{1}{4}$	$\frac{1}{8}$	$\frac{1}{16}$
Relative intensity ...	1	$\frac{1}{4}$	$\frac{1}{16}$	$\frac{1}{64}$	$\frac{1}{256}$
Relative exposure ...	1	4	16	64	256

Instead of marking each aperture with its fractional diameter, or its ratio aperture, we may mark it, either with its relative intensity or its relative exposure. Both systems of marking are in use, but the advantage of marking the intensity is very problematical, while that of marking the exposure is more apparent than real. If either system is adopted it is evident an aperture of $f/1$ is an inconvenient unit, as the numbers representing intensity and exposure soon expand into formidable values. Taking, for example, apertures $f/8$ and $f/16$: with $f/1$ as the unit the intensities are as $1/64 : 1/256$, and the exposures as 64 to 256. If we take $f/8$ as unity, then the intensities are as $1 : 1/4$ and the exposures as $1 : 4$. Further, the fractions representing intensity can be eliminated if we take the smallest instead of the largest stop as the unit; thus, if $f/16$ is the unit the intensities are as $4 : 1$. In all the recognised systems, a small aperture is the unit if intensities are marked; and a large one if the apertures are classified by exposure.

There are three systems of classification according to exposure; one known as the Uniform System (U.S.) of the Royal Photographic Society, in which an aperture of $f/4$ is taken as requiring a unit exposure. Another is the Dallmeyer System, in which $f3\cdot16$ gives a unit exposure. The third is the Continental or International System, also known as the C.I. system, in which $f/10$ requires a unit exposure. The two former are now practically obsolete, but the third is still in use. Then there are two Zeiss systems, in which apertures are classified according to intensity, $f/100$ having a unit intensity in the "old" system, and $f/50$ in the "new" system. These different systems with their varying units may cause a good deal of confusion. For example, a stop marked simply 4 may be under the U.S. system equal to $f/8$, or under Dallmeyer's System $f/6\cdot3$; under the Continental System $f/20$, under Zeiss' new system $f/25$, and under the old system $f/50$. It is necessary to know what system is adopted before interpreting the number. If the apertures are marked under the U.S. system, the Royal Photographic Society recommend that both the relative exposure number and the fractional diameter should be given. This is equally desirable with any system.

All these systems suffer through the adoption of fixed unit apertures. If the actual apertures do not form part of a series including the unit, or multiples of it, the advantages of the system are nullified by the awkwardness of the stop numbers.

All series of apertures should be arranged so that each aperture is half the area of the next larger one, and therefore requires double the exposure; but, unfortunately, this rule is not always observed. If the apertures are of unusual sizes, it may not be apparent that they are in proper progression, and then it is advantageous to mark them with the relative exposures as well as their fractional diameters, taking the largest, or most generally useful aperture as the unit. A similar mode of marking is desirable if the apertures are not in a proper order, and the largest aperture is very often not in regular series with the rest. The various methods of marking apertures are given in the Appendix, Tables E to H, and rules for finding numbers in Appendix I.

It can be easily understood that in all cases the effective aperture (Sec. 9), not simply the diaphragm aperture, should be recorded. The effective aperture varies in very approximately the same ratio as the diaphragm aperture, and hence the latter may be sufficient if we only want to consider aperture from a relative point of view; but at times the actual effective aperture is absolutely necessary, and if the diaphragm aperture is substituted for it errors must arise. Unfortunately, lens makers seem to have no uniform system, some marking effective aperture and others only the diaphragm aperture. The actual aperture should be tested by the owner of a lens in the way that will be described in the chapter on measuring lenses.

It may also be added that apertures are often marked in a very approximate manner. Thus we frequently hear of aperture f 11, but possibly such an aperture is never used. It is usually f 11·3, but may be f 10·9, or f 11·1·8.

66. UNIFORMITY OF ILLUMINATION.—Strictly speaking, the intensity of illumination is greatest in the centre of the image, and falls off more or less from the centre to the edges of the plate. This lack of uniformity is quite apart from the question of flare, and is due to several causes.

First, to the fact that oblique light produces less effect
upon the film than direct light, owing to there being a
greater loss by reflection from the film and from the lens
surfaces. Second, oblique pencils, passing through a lens
or circular aperture, are smaller in sectional area than
direct pencils; they are of necessity narrower in primary
plane and therefore contain less light. Any of the diagrams
showing oblique pencils will illustrate this fact. Third,
oblique pencils are liable to be further reduced in area
owing to obstruction offered by the lens mount. The first
and second causes only will operate in the case of a single

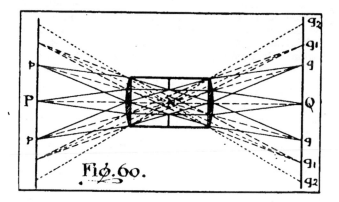

Fig. 60.

lens mounted in an aperture in a plane screen; the third,
if the lens is mounted in the usual way in a tube.

The falling off in uniformity of illumination owing to the
first two causes is gradual and continuous, but very slight
and practically negligible, excepting when pencils of very
great obliquity are in question. A mechanical limit is,
however, set to the employment of very oblique pencils by
the third cause of unequal illumination; that is, by the
construction and mounting of the lens which produces
very marked effects within certain fixed limits.

67. ANGLES AND CIRCLES OF ILLUMINATION.—In fig. 60
we show a doublet, and the pencils *pq* represent the most
oblique pencils that can pass through the lens without

being in any way obstructed by the lens mount. These pencils are narrower than the direct pencil PQ. and therefore in the image there is a slight falling off in illumination from Q to q owing to the second cause of inequality, and also a slight falling off in effect due to the first. Disregarding these two matters, however, the illumination from q to q is as complete and regular as the construction of the lens will permit, and the distance qq represents the diameter of a circle of complete illumination which is subtended by an angle of complete illumination $q N q$.

Light of greater obliquity can pass the lens, but the third cause of inequality then operates. An extreme limit is set to the illumination at the points q_2, which can only be reached by single theoretical rays, and thus $q_2 q_2$ is the diameter of a circle, and $q_2 N q_2$ is an angle, of extreme illumination. Between these angles of complete and extreme illumination, there is one, $q_1 N q_1$, bounded by pencils the sectional area of which is reduced one half by the obstruction of the lens mount. This is the angle of semi-illumination, and it subtends a circle of semi-illumination, the diameter of which is $q_1 q_1$. It should be noted that all three angles must be bisected by the principal axis of the lens.

The falling off in illumination from q to q_1 is at first slight, but it increases very rapidly. At q_1 there is a marked reduction of light, and beyond q_1 the loss is so rapid and so great that little effect is produced on the plate. Practically, all light effect ceases long before q_2 is reached. To avoid apparent inequality of illumination in the image, no part of it should be outside the circle of complete illumination ; but, as the diameter of this circle can be increased by reducing the aperture, it is possible to secure satisfactory illumination over a fairly large plate by sacrificing rapidity. From fig. 60 it is evident that while the extreme angle must be constant with any aperture, the use of an infinitely small aperture would make all three angles coincide; hence a reduction of aperture increases the angles of complete and semi-illumination. With a single landscape lens with diaphragm in front the angle of semi-illumination is practically constant for any aperture, and a reduction of aperture increases the angle of complete illumination and reduces that of extreme illumination.

As the aperture cannot be reduced below a certain size without inconveniently reducing the intensity, we cannot with any particular lens increase the circle of complete illumination beyond certain limits considerably short of those of the largest circle possible with a minute aperture. Thus, in fig. 60, with the smallest practicable aperture the angle of complete illumination must fall short of the angle $q_2 N q_2$. The extreme limiting angle can, however, be increased by bringing the lenses closer together, and this increases all the angles and converts a "narrow angle" lens into a relatively "wide angle" one. With a single landscape lens the angles can be similarly widened by bringing the diaphragm closer to the lens.

68. ANGLE AND CIRCLE OF DEFINITION.—Just as a lens has an angle and circle of complete illumination dependent on its mechanical construction, so it has an angle and circle of mean, or approximately uniform, definition, dependent on the extent to which oblique pencils are corrected for aberration, more particularly for .curvature and astigmatism. The angle of definition must be bisected by the principal axis similarly to the other angles.

Speaking generally, the size of the circle of definition increases as the aperture is diminished, but much, of course, depends on the nature of the uncorrected aberration and the degree to which it is effected by the aperture. A lens free from astigmatism and curvature will include a wider angle of definition than an astigmatic or curved field lens of the same aperture, and will include an equal angle at a larger aperture. In fact, lenses might well be classified in order of merit according to their angles of perfect definition at particular apertures. The best lens including the widest angle.

It may be noted that the shortening of the lens mount to increase the angle of illumination will either introduce aberration or render its correction more difficult, and the angle of definition cannot be very large if aberration is present. Obviously, uniform defining power is as important as uniformity of illumination, but it is not so easily secured, and at wide angles it cannot be expected except in lenses of the very highest class.

69. VIEW AND COVERING ANGLES.—The view angle may be defined as the angle subtended by the diagonal of the plate. This angle is only bisected by the principal axis when the plate is centrally opposite the lens. The covering angle may be defined as the angle subtending the diameter of the smallest circle that will include the plate within its limits; this angle always being bisected by the principal axis. When the plate is centred opposite the lens the view and covering angles coincide, but when the plate is not central the covering angle is necessarily greater than the view angle.

To secure even illumination and definition over the whole surface of the plate the covering angle must not exceed either the angle of complete illumination, or that of definition.

It should be noted that while the angles of illumination and definition limit the capabilities of the lens, the terms view and covering angles are only descriptive of the conditions under which the lens is used.

From Table J in the Appendix, we can find the angle covering a circle of definite diameter, and we can thus determine either the covering angle or the view angle included on a plate centrally opposite the lens. If the plate is not centred the table will give the covering angle, but will over estimate the view angle. Table K gives the diagonals of plates of various sizes.

70. WIDE AND NARROW ANGLE LENSES.—While the terms wide and narrow may be applied in a relative sense to any of the angles that have been described, the particular term, "wide angle lens" is generally used to convey the fact that the lens is constructed in such a manner as to permit the passage of very oblique light pencils; it thus applies only to illumination. We may assume that if the diameter of the circle of illumination is greater than the focal distance of the lens, or the angle is greater than about 53°, the lens has a wide angle; if the diameter is less than two thirds of the focal distance, or the angle is under 36°, the lens is narrow angled; and anything between the two is a mid angle lens. Or we may put it this way: if the

focal distance of the lens is less than the diameter of
the circle the angle is wide; if from one to one and a
half times the diameter, the angle is a mid angle; if
beyond one and a half times the diameter, the angle is
narrow.

Other angles may also be conveniently distinguished as
wide, medium, or narrow, when similar proportions are
observed between focal distance and diameter of circle subtended by the angle.

The angle of definition being independent of that of
illumination, while the two may be equal in a very narrow
angle lens, the angle of definition is always the smaller in a

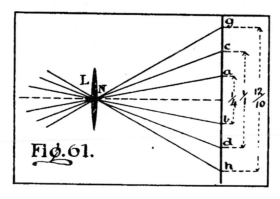

Fig. 61.

wide angle lens of similar aperture; hence a small aperture
is necessary if we wish to take advantage of the wide angle,
or, in other words, if we wish to employ a large covering
angle.

A wide angle lens may be of any focal length, but it
is evident that if we wish to include a wide view angle on
a small plate, we must use a lens of comparatively short
focal length. For example, assume that we have a wide
angle 8-in lens (*L* in fig. 61). A quarter plate *ab* will
subtend a narrow view angle, *aNb*; a whole plate *cd*
a medium view angle *cNd*; and a 12 × 10, *gh*, a wide
view angle *gNh*. The lens is of short focal length for the
12 × 10 plate, but of long focal length for the quarter plate.

To produce a wide angle view on the quarter plate we should require a wide angle lens of less than 4 in. in focal length.

Though the 8-in. lens will not include a wide view angle on a quarter plate, the position of the plate may necessarily produce a wide covering angle. If the rising front is used so that the quarter plate is at *bh*, the view angle *bNh* is still narrow, but the covering angle is increased to *gNh*. The altered relative position of the plate thus requires the insertion of a smaller diaphragm to produce satisfactory illumination and definition with the larger covering angle. Under these conditions we must have a wide angle lens, even though we are only making a narrow angle view, and as such a lens passes a great deal more light than is actually required, the image may suffer a certain amount of degradation through this surplus light being reflected on to the plate from the sides of the camera. To prevent this effect it is advisable to intercept the surplus light by means of a screen either in front of or behind the lens.

71. COVERING POWER.—The catalogue statement that a lens covers a certain angle or size of plate with a given aperture is somewhat indefinite. Sometimes it evidently is only true as regards illumination (not always complete illumination), and quite incorrect in respect to definition. The modern anastigmats will generally be found to cover with complete illumination and good definition the whole surface of the plate they are listed to cover; but this is by no means the case with the cheaper and less perfectly corrected lenses, and purchasers should be careful to test the point. It should, however, be understood that many cheap lenses produce excellent results with fair rapidity if used only for narrow covering angles; in fact we may say that any lens will produce good results within a certain limited angle, but with a poor lens the angle is very small. To render this quite clear, a cheap rectilinear may within an angle of 30° produce an image equal in all respects to that formed by an expensive anastigmat of the same rapidity; but increase the angle to 50°, and while the rectilinear has to be severely stopped down, the anastigmat is just as efficient as before, and

it will probably remain so if the angle is increased to 70°. Emphasis is laid upon this matter, because many seem to think that a cheap lens must be inferior to an expensive one under all conditions, and colour is given to this belief by the fact that the cheap lens will seldom perform well at the angle that the catalogue states it will " cover."

Some catalogues give the "covering angle" in degrees; some give the diameter of the circle subtended by the angle; and others only the size of the plate that can be included in that circle. Occasionally, however, they give what they call the *angular aperture* in degrees; meaning, probably, the angle of illumination. This is a misuse of a term which is often used in quite a different sense; see footnote to Sec. 64.

CHAPTER VII.

DEPTH.

72. DEPTH.—Under the laws of conjugate foci, when a point P (fig. 62) is at a certain distance u from the lens L, an absolutely sharp image of that point can only be obtained at the point Q, at a distance v from the lens; and, conversely, if the focussing-screen is fixed at Q, P is the only point that will be represented in absolutely sharp focus.

It is, however, manifest that a focus such as Q may be blurred to a certain slight extent, without that fact becoming noticeable. Therefore, either the screen or the object may suffer a certain amount of displacement without the production of appreciable blur. For example, the screen may be anywhere between, say, q_1 and q_2 without throwing the image of P obviously out of focus, and P may be anywhere between, say, P_1 and P_2 and still be represented with sufficient sharpness on a screen at Q.

The points P_1, P_2 limit depth of field, while q_1, q_2 limit depth of definition, and it is necessary to clearly understand the distinction between depth of field and definition.

Depth of field gives the limits of all axially situated object points that can be simultaneously represented in approximate sharp focus, when P is sharply defined on a screen at Q.

Depth of definition limits the permissible position of the screen, if it is desired to keep P in approximate focus.

When photographing a solid object we consider depth of field, but if the object is plane we mainly consider depth of definition, which must obviously affect focussing, the use of the swing back, and the scale of the image.

110

Depth of field is always considered relatively to the position of P; depth of definition relatively to Q, the conjugate focus of P.

The points q_1, q_2 are not conjugates to, nor have they any definite relationship with P_1 and P_2, but still, depth of field and definition are in a way connected. Assume Q_1 and Q_2 to be the conjugate foci to P_1 and P_2, so that P_2 will be sharp with the screen at Q_2, and P_1 be in focus with the screen at Q_1. If then P_1 and P_2 limit the depth of field when we focus on P with the screen at Q, it follows that Q must limit the front depth of definition for Q_2 and the back depth for Q_1. The points Q_1 and Q_2, though near, are quite distinct from the points

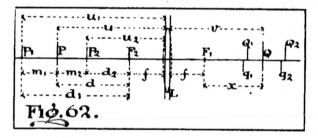

FIG. 62.

q_1 and q_2, which limit the front and back depth of definition for Q.

The distinction between the terms "depth of field" and "depth of definition" is not always strictly observed. The latter term (and also "depth of focus") is frequently applied to matters that solely relate to depth of field, which is also sometimes called "depth of distance."

Depth is a matter of importance in either direct or oblique pencils, but only with the former is it possible to arrive at practically useful formulæ, unless we assume the lens to be so perfect as to produce under all conditions a plane image from a plane object; in which case the formulæ applying to direct pencils cover oblique ones also, if all measurements are taken on, or parallel to, the principal axis. If curvature of the field exists, depth in oblique pencils can only be considered in a generally vague manner, and as it concerns the whole image or object, or what we may call the focal volume of the image or object. Thus there are four matters to consider—"depth of field," "depth of definition," "definition volume," and "field volume."

73. THE CIRCLE OF CONFUSION.—The amount of any kind of depth is dependent on the amount of out-of-focus blur that may be deemed to be permissible. This varies, under certain conditions dependent on the subject, size, and purpose of the photograph, but, as a general rule, we may allow $\frac{1}{100}$ in. as a maximum. This means that the image of an infinitely small object point (or of an infinitely thin line), is considered to be in adequately sharp focus so long as its breadth does not exceed $\frac{1}{100}$ in., or that sufficient sharpness is secured so long as the image of any larger point is not widened to a greater extent than $\frac{1}{100}$ in. That dimension may then be described as the maximum diameter of the permissible circle or disc of confusion that will adequately represent an infinitely small point.

It should be remembered that if the image is subsequently enlarged any out-of-focus effect is also enlarged, and while an amount of confusion of $\frac{1}{100}$ in. may be of no consequence in a direct print, an enlargement of four diameters will show a blur of $\frac{1}{25}$ in. which may be very detrimental. If an effect of extreme sharp focus is desired, $\frac{1}{100}$ in. blur is too much in a small print, and it may be reduced to $\frac{1}{250}$ in. with advantage. It may further be noted that a certain amount of blur is inevitable when objects at widely varying distances are included in the one image, hence, in view of future enlargement, it is important to ensure perfect focus on the most important part of the subject. If this precaution is not taken it may be found that in the enlarged image sharp definition exists only in the less important features of the view.

For the sake of explaining matters connected with depth we need only consider the effect of allowing a circle of confusion of $\frac{1}{100}$ in. but it must be understood that this factor is subject to modification.

74. MEASUREMENT OF DEPTH.—The positions of the points limiting depth may be denoted in several ways.

Consider, for example, the matter of depth of field as illustrated in fig. 62, in which the total depth of field for the point P (or the distance u) is denoted by the distance P_1P_2. This may be divided into near depth of field PP_2, or far depth of field P_1P (m_2 and m_1). Or we may fix P_1 and P_2 by taking their focal distances from the lens, u_2 being the near focal depth and u_1 the far focal depth of field. Or, again, we may take the extra-focal distance from F^2, the front principal focus of the lens; P_2F_2 (d_2) is then the near, and P_1F_2 (d_1) the far extra-focal depth. Sometimes one mode of expression is more convenient than the other; but, generally, the focal depths may be considered as of first importance for depth of field, while in the case of depth of definition we need consider only the total depth q_1q_2, or the front depth q_1Q and the back depth Qq_2.

It will be obvious that when we know u and its near or far focal depth of field, the difference between the two dimensions gives the near or far depth, while by deducting the focal-length of the lens from the focal depth we get the extra-focal depth.

75. AXIAL DEPTH OF FIELD.—The factors that have to be considered are four : the distance of the point P on which we sharply focus, which may be expressed either by the focal distance u, or the extra-focal distance d; the focal length of the lens, expressed by f; the diameter of the effective aperture, which may be expressed by its nominal fractional diameter of f/a; and the diameter of the disc of permissible confusion, which we assume to equal $\frac{1}{100}$ in. (It is important to note that the effective, and not the diaphragm aperture must be taken.) With any particular lens and aperture the last three factors are constants, and in the formulæ they appear invariably in one form, which may be termed the depth constant of the lens for that particular aperture. This depth constant is represented by H, and it is always equal to $100f^2/a$, or to the focal length multiplied into the diameter of the aperture and divided by the diameter of the circle of confusion. Knowing the value of H (see Appendix, Table L) for a particular aperture, depth of field can be calculated by the aid of very simple

8

formulæ that can be easily remembered. In exact formulæ we must employ both the focal distance u and the extra-focal distance d, but when comparatively long distances are in question the difference between u and d may well be disregarded.

It should be noted that H varies directly with the diameter of the aperture, and with the focal length, while it varies inversely with the diameter of the circle of confusion.

All the formulæ relating to depth of field for a point P at a focal distance u, or at an extra-focal distance d, may be collected in a tabulated form as follows :

DEPTH OF FIELD.

	NEAR DEPTHS.		FAR DEPTHS.	
Focal depth ...	$u_2 = \dfrac{uH}{H+d}$	... (23)	$u_1 = \dfrac{uH}{H-d}$	... (24).
Extra-focal depth	$d_2 = \dfrac{d(H-f)}{H+d}$	(25)	$d_1 = \dfrac{d(H+f)}{H-d}$	(26).
Depth	$m_2 = \dfrac{du}{H+d}$	... (27)	$m_1 = \dfrac{du}{H-d}$	... (28).

The distances u_2, u_1 and u, are in harmonic progression, and therefore—

$$\frac{1}{u_2} + \frac{1}{u_1} = \frac{2}{u} \quad \dots \quad \dots \quad \dots \quad (29).$$

The depths m_2 and m_1, are connected by the formula

$$\frac{1}{m_2} - \frac{1}{m_1} = \frac{2}{u} \quad \dots \quad \dots \quad \dots \quad (30).$$

The application of these formulæ is very simple. Suppose, for example, we have a lens of 6 ins. focal length and aperture f10. The depth constant $= 100f^2/a = 360$ ins. or 30 ft. If now we focus on a distance of 10 ft. the near focal depth of field equals $360 \times 120 \div (360 + 114) = 7$ ft. 7 ins. about, while the far focal depth of field $= 360 \times 120 \div (360 - 114) = 14$ ft. $7\frac{1}{2}$ ins. about. From these results it is evident, without applying formulæ 27 and 28, that the near depth of field is 2 ft. 5 ins. while the far depth is 4 ft. $7\frac{1}{2}$ ins.

The application of formulæ 25 to 28 is equally simple, but 23 and 24 are, in ordinary cases, the only ones required, and they may be easily remembered. We may, however, disregard the difference between u and d, if these dimensions are large compared with f, and then we have the still simpler formulæ:

$$u_2 = \frac{uH}{H + u} \quad (31); \text{ and } u_1 = \frac{uH}{H - u} \quad \dots \quad (32).$$

In words. The near focal depth of field is approximately equal to the product of the distance into the constant, divided by their sum; and the far focal depth, the product of the distance into the constant, divided by their difference. Extra-focal distances may be substituted for focal distances if desired in these approximate formulæ.

Formula 29 is useful for an altogether different purpose. Assume that we want to find the intermediate distance on which we should focus between two known distances u_1, and u_2, both of which are to be equally well defined. From the formula it is evident that

$$u = \frac{2u_1 u_2}{u_1 + u_2} \quad \dots \quad \dots \quad \dots \quad (33);$$

and assuming the subject to extend from 10 to 40 ft. from the lens, the nearest and farthest objects are equally well defined if we focus on a distance equal to $2 \times 40 \times 10 \div (40 + 10) = 16$ ft.

The confusion of the near and distant points will then be equal to 1/100 in. if

$$a = 100 f^2 \frac{u - u_2}{u_2 d} \text{ or } 100 f^2 \frac{u_1 - u}{u_1 d} \quad \dots \quad \dots \quad (34).$$

If f is equal to 6 ins., a must be 11·6, or the aperture must not exceed $f/11·6$.

The last problem is somewhat unusual, and formulæ 33 and 34 are seldom required.

In regard to the focal depths of field given in formulæ 23 and 24 there are two special cases to consider. If u is infinite, only near depth of field exists, and the near focal depth then is equal to H.

In the previous example $H = 30$ ft. hence when we focus on infinity the nearest object in approximate focus must be at a focal distance of 30 ft. from the lens; or all objects beyond 30 ft. must be in focus.

The second case is this : from formula 24 it is evident that if $d = H$ then the far depth of field is infinite ; therefore, if we focus on a focal distance u equal to $H + f$, all objects beyond that distance are in focus. If now we substitute $H + f$ for u and H for d in formula 23, we find that the near focal depth equals $\frac{1}{2} (H + f)$, just half the distance u. All objects beyond a distance of $\frac{1}{2} (H + f)$ are therefore in focus, and the depth of field ranges from $\frac{1}{2} (H + f)$ up to infinity. This is the maximum amount of depth of field possible, and $H + f$ may be styled the distance of maximum depth of field. If we measure this distance extra-focally it is equal to H, and is sometimes called the hyperfocal distance. The depth constant and hyperfocal distance are quite distinct, though of the same value. (Table K serves as a table of hyperfocal distance.)

It is sometimes found that depths calculated for a near distance do not appear to be strictly accurate when practically tested, even though the exact formulæ are used. This apparent error may be due to several causes. The focal length and the effective aperture must both be exactly known to find H, and very often neither is known with sufficient accuracy. Further, the diameter of the aperture may be correct only for a very distant object, and not for a near one. This is a likely source of error with a single lens. Then again it is not always easy to determine the exact distance of the point in sharp focus. All these causes may contribute to produce a fairly considerable error when focussing on an object only a few feet from the lens, and it is not advisable to trust too much to calculated depth in such cases. Very commonly the apparent error is due to the fact that the object lies in a portion of the field volume to which the calculated axial depths do not apply. This will be again referred to.

It should be observed that the formulæ given are true only for axial depth of field in the case of a lens that is capable of producing a perfect focus, and that they represent the maximum possible amount of depth. Any form of aberration that deteriorates the focus reduces depth ; hence the better the correction of the lens the

greater is the depth. The exact effect of aberration on depth
cannot be allowed for in formulæ, hence depth must be a
somewhat uncertain quantity in a poor lens. It is a common
error to suppose that depth is increased by the presence of
aberration ; the exact contrary is the case. The mistake is
due to the fact that if the lens will not produce perfect
definition under any conditions, we naturally make
allowance for a circle of confusion that is much larger than
$\frac{1}{100}$ in. No formulæ are applicable in such a case, and
the matter is purely one of personal judgment. The lack of
a critically sharp standard of definition aids to produce an
appearance of great depth that is very deceptive in a
small image. Enlargement will prove that this pseudo-
depth is only universal bad definition. A little consideration will show that if a lens cannot represent a point
without a blur of $\frac{1}{100}$ in. there is absolutely no depth at
all, unless we allow a permissible disc of confusion larger
than $\frac{1}{100}$ in.

76. CONSECUTIVE DEPTHS OF FIELD.—A question that often
arises in regard to depth of field is this. If the nearest
and farthest points in focus are P_2 and P_1 when focussing
sharply on P, will P remain in focus if we focus sharply
on either P_1 or P_2 ? Or, in other words, does P limit the
near depth of field for P_1 and the far depth of field for P_2?
As a matter of fact, what has already been said with regard
to the connection between depth of field and definition
shows that these conditions are not fulfilled ; but practically
they are very nearly so, and it is possible to select a
continuous series of distances in which each point shall
very approximately represent the near depth of field of the
next point on one side, and the far depth of field of the
next point on the other, the error in depth never exceeding
one focal length. For this purpose it is advisable to
measure all distances extra-focally, and the required conditions are fulfilled, so long as any three distances are in
the order $H \div (n-1)$, $H \div n$, $H \div (n+1)$; or by the continuous series.

$$\left.\begin{array}{l}\text{Infinity,} \quad H, \quad H/2, \quad H/3, \quad H/4, \quad H/5, \quad \text{etc.}\\ \text{or}\\ \text{Infinity, } 100f^2/a,\ 100f^2/2a,\ 100f^2/3a,\ 100f^2/4a,\ 100f^2/5a,\ \text{etc.}\end{array}\right\}(35).$$

The truth of this can be tested readily. Assume

we focus on an extra-focal distance equal to H/n. Substituting H/n, for d in formulæ 25 and 26 we find that the near extra-focal depth is $(H-f) \div (n+1)$, and the far extra-focal depth is $(H+f) \div (n-1)$. If for the former we substitute $H \div (n+1)$, the result is too great by an amount equal to only $f \div (n+1)$. If for the far depth we employ $H \div (n-1)$ the result is too small by $f \div (n-1)$. Both errors are on the safe side and from their smallness are of no possible consequence.

As an example suppose we have a 6-in. lens working at $f10$. H then equals 360 ins. or 30 ft. Assume we focus on a distance d equal to $H/3$ or 10 ft. The near extra-focal depth by the accurate formula is equal to $(H-f) \div (n+1) = (360-6) \div (3+1) = 88\frac{1}{2}$ ins. By the approximate formula $H \div (n+1)$ it equals $360/4 = 90$ ins. There is then an error on the safe side of $1\frac{1}{2}$ ins. Taking the far depth by the accurate formula it equals $(H+f) \div (n-1) = (360+6) \div (3-1) = 183$ ins. By the approximate formula it equals $H \div (n-1) = 360/2 = 180$ ins. The error is here 3 ins. on the safe side. The maximum possible error in near depth exists when d is infinite and $n = 0$, the error then being f. When focussing on a distance $H/2$ the far depth is in error by one focal length. The error would be greater than this if focussing on a distance between $H/2$ and H, but such a distance is not included in the series, and, anyway, the error is insignificant compared with the distance of far depth, which is infinite when focussing on H.

A series of distances of consecutive depth may very conveniently be selected for dividing a focussing scale. (Consecutive depths for an aperture of $f8$ and various focal lengths are given in Table M, see Appendix.)

77. VARIATIONS IN DEPTH OF FIELD.—All lenses give the same amount of depth of field for a given distance, so long as their depth constants are the same ; but the greater the constant the less the depth, and *vice versa*. Assuming that in all cases we allow a circle of confusion of $\frac{1}{100}$ in., then the value of H, which equals $f^2/a \times 100$, varies with that of f^2/a. If we reduce the aperture alone, keeping f constant, a is increased, H diminished, and depth increased. If we reduce the focal length, keeping f/a, or the diameter

of the aperture, constant, H diminishes with f, and depth increases. If we preserve the ratio aperture, or $1/a$, constant, and reduce f, H diminishes with f^2, and depth increases rapidly.

To preserve constant depth a must vary with f^2; that is, if we double f, a must be multiplied by 4, which process halves the diameter of the aperture. Here we have assumed that the circle of confusion is of constant diameter. Some have, however, advocated the varying of this factor in proportion to the focal length of the lens, so that the amount of confusion may vary more or less with the scale of the image. This gives a constant value to the quotient of the focal length divided by the diameter of the circle of confusion, and leaves H to vary only with the diameter of the aperture. Thus the depth remains constant for any particular distance with an aperture of, say, 1 in., for a lens of any focal length. To gain any idea of the actual amount of depth we must, however, fix a certain amount of confusion for a lens of particular focal length, and calculate the depths with apertures of various diameters for a certain scale of distances.

It can be easily understood that this system is inconvenient if obvious confusion is undesirable in large scale images, and extremely acute definition is not wanted in small ones. If we permit $\frac{1}{50}$ in. confusion with a 16-in. lens we can only allow $\frac{1}{200}$ in. with a 4-in. lens, and this, perhaps, excessively fine definition is attained at the expense of depth that might otherwise be taken advantage of. While it may be desirable in pictorial work that definition should vary somewhat with the scale, it is inconvenient to vary it strictly in the ratio of the scale. The circle of confusion and the depth constant should be varied solely in accordance with the necessities of the work, without following any arbitrary rule.

78. AXIAL DEPTH OF DEFINITION.—As with depth of field, we must fix upon a maximum permissible amount of confusion, say $\frac{1}{100}$ in., and we may also conveniently adopt a definition constant to simplify the formulæ.

Referring to fig. 62, front depth of definition is measured by the distance q_1Q and back depth by Qq_2. Under all circumstances front and back depth are equal, therefore one formula applies to both. The factors affecting axial depth of definition are ;—the focal distance of the true focus from the lens, or the distance v, which is conjugate to u ; the diameter of the circle of confusion, which we assume to be $\frac{1}{100}$ in.; and the diameter of the lens aperture, which may be expressed by its nominal fractional diameter of f/a. If we divide the diameter of the circle of confusion by the diameter of the aperture we obtain a definition constant h, which has only to be multiplied by v to obtain the depth of definition for any value of v. Thus depth of definition is always equal to

$$ hv = \frac{av}{100f} \qquad \ldots \qquad \ldots \qquad \ldots \qquad (36). $$

It may be noted that if we allow the same amount of confusion for either depth of field or depth of definition, then the depth constant h is equal to the focal length of the lens divided by the depth constant H. Thus $h = f/H = a/100f$.

Assume that we have a 5-in. lens with aperture $f10$, or $\frac{1}{2}$ in. in diameter. The depth constant $H = 250$ ins. The definition constant $= \frac{5}{250}$. in. $= \frac{1}{50}$ in. Or, it equals $\frac{1}{100}$ in. $\div \frac{1}{2} = \frac{1}{50}$ in. If we focus on a distant object so that $v = f$, the front or back depth of definition is equal to $\frac{5}{50}$ in. or ·1-in. If we focus on a near object so that $v = 6$ ins., the depth of definition $= \frac{6}{50}$ or ·12 in. If we are copying full size $v = 2f$ and the depth is ·2 in. If enlarging on a scale of 4 to 1, $v = 5f$ and the front or back depth of definition is ·5 in., while the total depth is 1 in.

It is manifest that the amount of depth varies directly with the value of h. That is, inversely with the size of the aperture, and directly with the size of the circle of confusion. Thus, if in the above example we substitute aperture $f20$ for $f10$ the total depth of definition, when we enlarge four times, is increased to 2 ins. If, on the other hand, we only allow $\frac{1}{200}$ in. confusion, the total depth is reduced to $\frac{1}{2}$ in.

79. Focussing.—When the depth of definition is great there is obviously a difficulty in focussing accurately on a given object. Take the example of enlarging four times with a 5-in. lens and $f10$ aperture. If the aperture

cannot be increased the depth of definition is $\frac{1}{2}$-in. front or back of the true focus. One hundredth of an inch is, however, a very appreciable dimension, and we are not likely to place the focussing-screen as far as $\frac{1}{2}$ in. out of position; but if it is only $\frac{1}{8}$ in. out the blur is only $\frac{1}{100}$ in. and may escape notice, so the screen may be left anywhere within $\frac{1}{8}$ in. of the true position. If, then, we employ a magnifying glass that multiplies twice, the blur of $\frac{1}{100}$ in. is magnified to $\frac{1}{200}$ in. and becomes more appreciable, so that we can then place the screen within, say $\frac{1}{16}$ in. of the proper position. A more powerful magnifier will assist still further, but it should be noticed that the use of a ground-glass screen greatly interferes with the use of a focussing-magnifier. A clear glass screen should be used and the magnifier should be focussed carefully on the front surface of the screen.

A very near approach to accuracy is obtained by averaging the position of the screen. By racking in the screen until a recognisable amount of blur is produced we can find the limit of front depth of definition for a certain amount of confusion. If then we rack out the screen behind the true focus until we arrive at an equal amount of confusion, the screen is at the limit of back depth, and half-way between these two limits is the position for accurate focus. This is the proper method of focussing under any conditions.

As depth of definition varies inversely with the size of the aperture, it is easier to focus on near objects with a large aperture, than with a small one; but if the lens is not entirely free from longitudinal spherical aberration in direct pencils the after reduction of the aperture for exposure will throw the image out of focus.

80. DEPTH OF DEFINITION AND SCALE.—If a very small aperture is used the depth of definition may be so increased as to not only render it difficult to place the screen at the one true focus, but to even render it immaterial, so far as focus is concerned, whether the screen is there or not. Suppose, for example, that we have a 5-in. lens with an aperture of $\frac{1}{40}$ in.; that is, $f/200$, and that we consider a confusion of $\frac{1}{200}$ in. to be imperceptible. The definition constant is then $\frac{1}{200} \div \frac{1}{40} = \frac{1}{5}$, and when

the object is distant, so that the true value of v is f, we have a total depth of definition of 2 ins. The plate may then be anywhere between 4 and 6 ins. from the lens, the latter position giving a larger image than the former one. Practically we can obtain the same effects with the 5-in. lens as we could with either a 4- or 6-in. lens, so far as scale and view-angle are concerned. It must, however, be remembered that images produced in the extreme positions will not bear much, if any, enlargement, no part being in true focus. The question of depth of field does not come in, as the extremely small aperture renders it practically unlimited. The use of minute apertures to increase depth of definition to an extent sufficient to permit the production of varying size images was apparently first suggested by the Rev. F. C. Lambert.

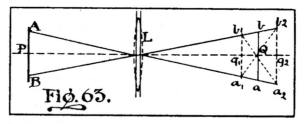

81. DEFINITION VOLUME.—Assume that we have a lens L (fig. 63) perfectly corrected in all respects and with an absolutely flat field. If q_1, q_2 limit the axial depth of definition for an object at P, then verticals a_1b_1 and a_2b_2, drawn through q_1 and q_2, will limit the depths of definition, b_1b_2 and a_1a_2, in oblique pencils Aa and Bb coming from a vertical object APB. If the object is plane and parallel to the focussing-screen then a_1b_1 and a_2b_2 may be looked upon as the traces of similar parallel planes which form the boundaries of a space called the definition volume. No part of the image will then be obviously out of focus if the focussing-screen is anywhere within this definition volume. Perfect focus is attained only in the position aQb, but approximate focus is secured even if the screen is inclined in the direction a_1b_2, or in that of a_2b_1, though the image is then distorted.

We do not, however, often come across a lens with an
ideal definition volume such as that illustrated. If the
lens has a curved field, as indicated by the dotted curve
passing through Q in fig. 64, the boundaries of the definition
volume are curved; and if the oblique pencils are astigmatic,
or in any way less perfectly corrected than direct pencils,
they have less depth of definition, and the definition volume
is so contracted that a section of it may take the form
shown by the thick curved lines. In this case we may have
a full amount of depth of definition on the axis which
cannot be taken advantage of, for if the plate is at q_2 the

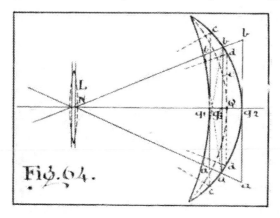

Fig. 64.

points a and b are outside the definition volume and out of
focus. To bring them into focus the plate would have to
be at q_3 in front of Q, hence the depth of definition is
practically limited to $q_1 q_3$, while the inclination of the
plate may not exceed that shown by the dotted lines. It
will be noticed that the angle of definition is affected by the
position of the plate. If at q, the angle cNc is at a
maximum; if at q_2 the angle is almost nil, and at Q, dNd
is too small to include a and b. The best average definition
is obtained at q_3, but in that position it is evident that the
best possible focus is secured about e, where the plate
intersects the curved field of mean focus. In the image
there is therefore likely to be a circular zone of superior

definition concentric to the central axial point, which, in
order to compromise matters, has been thrown slightly out
of focus. This sort of compromise has often to be effected
with inferior lenses, but the reason for it must not be
confounded with that for adopting a similar method of
excentric focussing with some of the anastigmats, which
are so constructed as to produce, under any circumstances,
the best definition a little way from the centre.

It is obvious that as depth of definition is increased by
reducing the aperture, the definition volume is also increased.
A small aperture is invariably a remedy for deficiency of
any kind of depth.

82. Use of Swingback.—We have referred to the fact

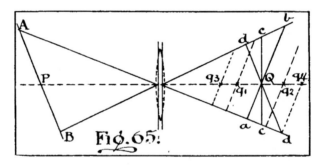

Fig. 65.

that while the plate may be inclined from the vertical
within the definition volume without destroying focus, such
a proceeding produces distortion. Conventionally we look
upon all images as distorted when taken upon non-vertical
plates, even though they are in perfectly true plane
perspective.

When we tilt the camera to take in a high vertical
building, distortion is produced if the plate is not adjusted
to a vertical position. The upper part of the building is
then farther from the lens than the lower part, and its
image is nearer the lens, therefore the true image of the
whole lies on a plane inclined away from the lens in an
opposite direction to that of the object. This is illustrated
in fig. 65 where for convenience the principal axis of

the lens is kept horizontal while the object AB is tilted. If the paper is turned so as to make AB vertical, it will be seen that the diagram reproduces the effect of taking a high vertical object with a tilted camera. The point B in the object being nearer the lens than A, b in the image is farther from the lens than a.

The lens being perfectly corrected, the definition volume of the true image may be represented by the dotted lines passing through q_1, q_2. Suppose now the plate to be in the position cQc, at right angles to the principal axis. The image on the non-vertical plate is distorted, but in fair focus, the plate being inside the definition volume.* To cure the distortion we must incline the plate in the direction dd parallel to AB and therefore vertical, which throws the plate outside the definition volume and out of focus. To remedy distortion and preserve focus we must reduce the aperture to a sufficient extent to increase the depth of definition to q_3q_4.

This is an example of the use of the swingback to obviate distortion. If, however, slight distortion is of no consequence, we may leave the plate just within the definition volume of the true image and so secure good focus with a large aperture. A better remedy is to increase the distance between the object and the lens, this alters the slope of the true image, and brings the plate within its definition volume.

83. FIELD VOLUME.—We have here only considered the matter of definition volume as it applies to a plane object. It should be understood that from a solid object a lens projects a solid aerial image ; that is to say, if the object is a cube the true image is a cube. If we focus sharply on a given point the whole will be in approximate focus if the plate is within the definition volume of every separate part of the solid aerial image, and then the whole of the object must of necessity be within the field volume of the plane in sharp focus. The field volume may vary in much the same way as the definition volume, but it may be noted that if the lens has a field with positive curvature for a plane object,

---

* This is the case in the diagram. In practice, part of the plate might be outside the definition volume, and, therefore, out-of-focus.

it has a plane field for an object that is concave to the lens. Hence the near boundary of the field volume is also concave to the lens, and objects lying well off the principal axis may be within the field volume though apparently they are too near the lens to be within the depth of field measured axially. Thus in a group of persons sitting in a semicircle the outer ones may be in focus though they appear nearer to the lens than the axial point that is the nearest in focus. In other words, there is greater near depth of field at the margins of the view than in the centre. This is not unfrequently the case, though too often any advantage in this respect is counteracted by aberrations in the oblique pencils. The form of the field volume, as of the definition volume, is a variable feature, and it is only possible to obtain an idea of it by experiment. In the ideal lens it should be remembered both volumes are bounded by planes. If bounded by curved surfaces we must be prepared to find that the axial depth formulæ give erroneous ideas of the depth that is really available. Thus if the boundaries are concave to the lens, far depth of field and back depth of definition suffer, and if the boundaries are convex to the lens, near depth of field and front depth of definition are practically less than the formulæ appear to indicate.

CHAPTER VIII.

84. FOCUSSING-SCALES.—Instead of focussing visually on the ground glass screen, we may measure or estimate the distance of the object and then adjust the screen by predetermined marks corresponding to particular distances. A series of such marks form a focussing-scale, and there are two matters for consideration in connection with such scales ; first, the manner in which the positions of the scale marks are determined ; and second, the particular distances that they should represent. The simplest way to determine the exact position of the screen for an object at a given distance is to set up an object at that distance, focus upon it, and record the position of the screen ; but this is only practically convenient when focussing on an infinite distance, or on one that is easily measured. With intermediate distances that are too great to be measured and too small to be infinite, the extension of the camera must be calculated and set off from some convenient datum.

85. THE INFINITY MARK.—The most convenient datum point from which the scale can be set out is the infinity mark, which can be found as follows. Focus as carefully and accurately as possible on some object at an infinite distance, and then mark in any convenient fixed spot the exact position of any moving portion of the camera that will serve as an index point, then, whenever we adjust the index to this infinity mark, the focussing-screen is at the principal focus of the lens. It is manifest that if we rack out the camera so that the index point is, say, 1 in. beyond the infinity mark, then the focussing-screen is also 1 in. behind the principal focus. Therefore, any distance measured from the infinity mark corresponds to an extra-focal distance measured from the principal focus.

To find the infinity mark we may focus on the sun or moon, but these are not generally convenient objects, and we may as well select some terrestrial object at a finite distance sufficiently great to render the error in the position of the screen negligible. Having fixed on a permissible amount of error, the nearest object on which we may focus is at an extra-focal distance equal to the square of the focal length divided by the error. Assuming we allow a displacement of the screen to the extent of $\frac{1}{100}$ in. the nearest distance of approximate infinity is $100f^2$, or if we allow only $\frac{1}{250}$ in. error the distance is $250f^2$, and so on. If the infinity mark is to serve as the datum of a scale, $\frac{1}{100}$ in. error is too great; but it is easy with short focus lenses to employ suitable objects at greater distances which will give a much smaller error. Thus, supposing we have a 6-in. lens and allow $\frac{1}{100}$ in. error we need only focus on an object 100 yds. away; but it is just as easy to select one 300 or 400 yds. off and so reduce the error to $\frac{1}{300}$ or $\frac{1}{400}$ in., or less. The formula only serves as a guide to the nearest permissible distance, and the farther we go beyond that distance the better.

(Table N in the Appendix gives distances of approximate infinity for lenses of various focal lengths.)

It will be of course evident that the infinity mark may be found if we can place the focussing-screen at the principal focus of the lens by any method other than that of focussing on a distant object.

86. DISTANCES SHORT OF INFINITY.—If we focus on a near object at an extra-focal distance d, we shall have to rack out the camera beyond the infinity mark for a distance equal to the conjugate extra-focal distance x, and from the formulæ relating to extra-focal distances (see Sec. 33) we know that $x = f^2/d$. Thus, if with a 6-in. lens we want to mark the scale for an object 6 ft. away from the front principal focus of the lens, we set out from the infinity mark a distance equal to $\frac{36}{72} = \frac{1}{2}$ in., and if then we adjust the moving index to that mark, an object

6 ft. away is in focus. It must be noted that x varies in inverse proportion with d; hence if d is doubled x is halved, and *vice versa*. Thus the mark for a distance of 12 ft. will be $\frac{1}{4}$ in. from the infinity mark, and that for a distance of 3 ft. will be 1 in. from the infinity mark. If such a mark proves to be incorrect, either there is an error in the focal length, or aberration in the lens is to blame. A test should be made on a near object at a carefully measured distance.

87. SELECTION OF DISTANCES.—The simplest possible form of mechanical focussing is adopted in the "fixed focus" camera, in which the lens should be fixed so as to produce a sharp image of an object at the hyperfocal distance of the largest diaphragm, and thus secure a maximum amount of depth of field (see Sec. 75). In such a case there is no focussing arrangement, all objects beyond a certain minimum distance, which can be reduced by diminishing the aperture, being always in focus. With a focussing-camera the hyperfocal distance should always be represented in the scale, and in many cases this distance takes the place of the true infinity mark which is omitted altogether. Practically the true infinity mark is not of much use, as it is seldom desirable to confine the sharpest definition to objects at an extreme distance; but if the hyperfocal distance takes the place of the infinity mark that fact should be known to the user of the camera. With different cameras there is unfortunately a great deal of uncertainty as to which mark is really shown, and sometimes it is to be feared that the extreme mark is neither one thing nor the other, but represents an intermediate distance, in which case it is of no use as a datum for setting out other marks. A distance equal to $100f$ is sometimes selected, but this distance is quite meaningless and represents nothing in particular. Assuming that we show the infinity mark and also the hyperfocal mark, for an aperture of f/a, then, as the hyperfocal distance, or H, equals $100f^2/a$, the two scale marks are separated by a distance equal to $f^2/H = a/100$.

Next the question arises as to shorter distances. These may be selected so as to provide a convenient series of dimensions, such as 5, 10, and 15 ft., but it is best to

9

adopt one of the more systematic arrangements that follow.

First, we may select the hyperfocal distances for each diaphragm or stop. Thus if with a 6-in. lens we have stops f8, 11, 16, 22, 32, 44, we might take the distances $100f^2/8$, $100f^2/11$, $100f^2/16$, $100f^2/22$, $100f^2/32$, $100f^2/44$, which equal approximately 37' 6", 27' 3", 18' 9", 13' 7", 9' 4", and 6' 9". Starting from the true infinity mark we should then have a series of divisions at the following distances from the datum, ·08, ·11, ·16, ·22, ·32, and ·44 in. The mark for 27' 3" would have to be omitted as it comes so close to the adjoining ones, and if we also omit the true infinity mark, and start with H for the hyperfocal distance of the largest aperture we shall have a scale as follows :

f8	f16	f22	f32	f44
H	18' 9"	13' 7"	9' 4"	6' 9"
or, H	19'	14'	$9\frac{1}{2}'$	7' approximately.

This is a fairly convenient series, and we can with any stop, except f11, focus at once upon the distance that gives maximum depth, or can tell what stop is required to give maximum depth at one of the distances. These are advantageous conditions in hand-camera work, but as all stops are not included it is advisable to mark each division with both the distance and the aperture to which it relates, as shown above. It should not be forgotten that the exact distances are extra-focal, and that when we focus on one distance with its own stop the depth of field extends approximately from half that distance up to infinity.

The second system of dividing the scale has certain advantages over this last method. If we take a series of consecutive depths of field for the largest aperture (see Sec. 76) we can tell the depths of field at near distances, and also the hyperfocal distances for every alternate stop. Assume again that we have a 6-in. lens with a series of stops f8, f11, f16, f22, f32, f44, f64. Taking the consecutive depths for f8 we have the following series :

Infinity, $100f^2/8$, $100f^2/16$, $100f^2/24$, $100f^2/32$, $100f^2/40$, $100f^2/48$, $100f^2/56$, $100f^2/64$

or,

Infinity, $\underset{f8}{37'\ 6''}$, $\underset{f16}{18'\ 9''}$, $12'\ 6''$, $\underset{f32}{9'\ 4''}$, $7'\ 6''$, $6'\ 3''$, $5'\ 4\frac{1}{2}''$, $\underset{f64.}{4'\ 8\frac{1}{2}''}$

This series includes hyperfocal distances for $f8, f16, f32,$ and $f64$, as indicated, and while we can always take advantage of the maximum depth of field for one of those stops, we can also tell the actual depth given by one of them while focussing on one of the marked distances. Thus if we focus by the scale to 7 ft. 6 ins. ; with $f8$ the depth extends from 6 ft. 3 ins. to 9 ft. 4 ins., being indicated one division away on either side of the focus mark. If we use $f16$ the depths are marked two divisions away, thus focussing on 9 ft. 4 ins. with $f16$ the depth extends from 6 ft. 3 ins. to 18 ft. 9 ins. With $f32$ we take four divisions on either side and find the depth is from 4 ft. 8 ins. up to infinity. The number of divisions always varies with the value of a in the fraction f/a, which is the fractional diameter of the aperture. The scale divisions for such a series of distances are equally spaced, each space being equal to $a/100$, or ·08 in. in above example.

It will be noticed that depths are only shown for half the series of stops. We took $f8$ as the basis of the scale and therefore only $f16$, $f32$, and $f64$ can be provided for. We might have taken $f11$ as the basis, and then depths would have been correct for $f22$, $f44$, etc., and not for $f8$, $f16$, etc. With a series of stops the diameters, of which were f/a, $f/2a$, $f/3a$, $f/4a$, etc., depth would be shown for every aperture, 1, 2, 3, or 4 divisions away from the focus mark ; but stops are arranged in series according to their areas, not their diameters, and so it is impossible to provide for all. Intermediate divisions will, however, approximately represent depths for intermediate stops. It may be noted that $f8$, is about the largest stop that can well be provided for ; the larger the initial aperture the smaller are the divisions, and the scale becomes confused if the divisions are too minute. It is of course evident that the scale will serve with any aperture for simple focussing purposes, though it may not give correct depths.

With a scale of this kind it is best to record the stop
values on the moving portion of the camera, so that they
may come opposite the proper divisions when focussing
on a given distance.   The scale may be arranged, as
shown in fig. 66.   The portion marked *A*, which shows
distances, is affixed to the base board or non-moving part
of the camera; the part marked *B* to the moving portion.
The arrowhead on *B* is the index point, and the stop
values are marked on either side of it at proper distances.

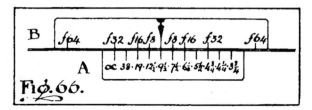

Fig. 66.

By setting the index point to a certain distance we secure
sharp focus on that distance.   If then we use one of
the particular stops marked we can read off the depth
of field at once.   As shown, sharp focus is secured on
9½ ft., and with stop *f*8 depth extends from 7½ to 12½ ft.;
with *f*16 from 6¼ to 19 ft.; with *f*32 from 4¾ ft. to infinity.
This indicates that 9½ ft. is the hyperfocal distance for *f*32,
and we can always obtain the maximum depth with
any stop by setting the stop value against the infinity
mark.

CHAPTER IX.

88. MEASURING LENSES.—In most calculations concerning lenses, focal length and aperture are most important factors, and to apply the results of such calculations it is generally necessary to know the positions of one or more of the cardinal points. Under the heading of measuring lenses we may therefore include the determination of the nodes, principal foci, focal length and aperture.

89. TO FIND THE PRINCIPAL FOCUS.—The most obvious method is that described for ascertaining the infinity mark for a focussing-scale. That is, to focus sharply upon an object at an infinite or approximately infinite distance, and note the position of the screen, which is then at the principal focus. Another method, applicable within the limits of an ordinary room is, however, sometimes useful. For the glass focussing-screen substitute an opaque screen with a small pinhole in the exact centre, and in front of the lens hood fix a diaphragm with an aperture of known dimensions, say $\frac{1}{2}$ in. in diameter. If a landscape lens is used the lens diaphragm will serve, but with a doublet an extra front diaphragm with an aperture smaller than that of the lens is essential. Some distance in front of the lens place a white screen, and behind the pinhole place a strong light. A disc of light will then be projected on to the screen. Adjust the distance between pinhole and lens until the projected disc is exactly the same size as the aperture in the front diaphragm. It is then evident that the emergent pencil of light is parallel, and therefore that the pinhole is at the principal focus. If the lens is well corrected for parallel light, the pinhole is

133

small, and the light intense, this method of finding the principal focus is fairly accurate and easily carried out.

When a lens is employed in this manner for the purpose of rendering the emergent light parallel it is styled a collimator, and it is fairly evident that if we have a camera, lens, and pinhole, so adjusted as to project a parallel beam of light, we can use this arrangement to find the principal focus of a second lens. Placing the second lens in the path of the parallel beam a sharp image of the pinhole will be formed at its principal focus. The collimator then serves the purpose of an infinitely distant source of light. Any camera and lens can be used as a collimator at a moment's notice, if the true infinity mark is known.

90. To FIND THE NODES.—If we know the principal foci and the focal length of a lens we can of course find the nodes by measuring back from the principal foci; and, conversely, if we know the nodes we can set out the focal length from them to find the principal foci. If, however, the focal length is unknown, the nodes must be independently found by taking advantage of the fact that the rotary centre coincides with the node of emission when the incident light is parallel. To do this we must be able to tentatively rotate the lens about various points on its principal axis until we find the rotary centre (see Sec. 26), and the operation is not easy without apparatus. The simplest method is to poise the lens on a sharp edge and rotate it horizontally; but strict accuracy requires the aid of the more elaborate apparatus styled a tourniquet, which is specially designed for the purpose.

91. To MEASURE FOCAL LENGTH.—If we know the principal foci and the nodes it is an easy matter to measure the focal length, which is the distance between them ; but we require the tourniquet to first find the nodes. Or again, if we can find the principal foci and the symmetric foci (see Sec. 34), the difference between them is the focal length ; but practically it is a very difficult matter to find the symmetric foci without the aid of apparatus such as Professor S. Thompson's focometer. We may guess at the position of the nodes, which in a rectilinear are not far from the diaphragm slot, or we may approximately find the symmetric foci by tentative adjustment of the camera ;

. but, either way, an uncertain amount of error is introduced which may vitiate future calculations. Methods of calculating focal lengths are therefore more generally useful than any attempt at measuring it without the aid of proper apparatus.

92. CALCULATING FOCAL LENGTH.—There are numerous methods of calculating focal length without determination of the nodes, and these methods may be divided into two classes : the approximate, in which the fact that a lens has usually two nodes is ignored ; and the theoretically accurate, in which that fact is taken into consideration. With some approximate methods the effect of this fundamental error is minimised, and, as in all cases we must allow a certain margin of error, it sometimes happens that a method that is not strictly correct in principle may yield as nearly a correct result as another method that, though theoretically correct, in practice favours the perpetration of errors in determining the preliminary data.

Approximate Methods of Calculating Focal Length.

(*a*) Focus an object on a scale of equal size and divide total distance from object to image by four. The result is the focal length *plus* or *minus* one quarter the nodal space. The object and image should each be at the symmetric foci, which are very difficult to find; additional error is therefore likely to be introduced by incorrect adjustment.

(*b*) The error in method *a*, due to ignoring the nodal space, may be diminished by copying on a reduced scale. Assume that the ratio of image to object, or the value of *R* is $1/n$. Let *D* equal the total distance of image from object, then the focal length =

$$f = \frac{Dn}{(n + 1)^2} \quad \cdots \quad \cdots \quad \cdots \quad (37).$$

The error due to the nodal space is then equal to *plus* or *minus* the product of the nodal space into $n \div (n+1)^2$. Say $R = \frac{1}{3}$ or $n = 3$, then the error is $\frac{3}{16}$ the nodal space. There is, however, with this method just as much difficulty in copying to an exact scale as in method *a*.

(*c*) The difficulty of copying on an exact scale may be got over by copying on any reduced scale an object of known dimensions ; afterwards finding the value of *n* by

comparing image with object and then applying the
formula.   In this case the object must be plane, and
parallel with the focussing-screen, otherwise fresh error
may be introduced.

(*d*) A method due to Mr. W. B. Coventry.   Mark
extension of camera when an object at an infinite distance
is sharply defined, and thus find the infinity mark.   Next,
focus on a near object and measure extension of camera
beyond infinity mark, calling this distance *x*.   Finally
measure distance from object to image and call it *D*.
Then

$$f = \sqrt{Dx} - x \quad \dots \quad \dots \quad \dots \quad (38);$$

or repeat operation with an object at a different distance,
and thus find two values for D (D and D_1) and two for x
(x and x_1).   Then

$$f = \frac{x(D - x) - x_1(D_1 - x_1)}{2(x - x_1)} \quad \dots \quad \dots \quad (39).$$

The error due to nodal space is very small if the value
of D is great, say over $10f$, and this method is perhaps
the best approximate one.   It, however, requires nearly
as many data as are sufficient to give a theoretically
correct result.

Theoretically Exact Methods.—With these, all dimensions
including the nodal space must be avoided, hence the
inclusive distance D cannot be employed.

(*e*) First find the infinity mark, then focus sharply on a
near object and measure the additional extension of the
camera beyond the infinity mark.   Call this distance *x*.
Next focus on a still nearer object and again measure
the extension of the camera beyond the infinity mark,
calling this distance *y*.   Let *B* equal the difference in
distance of the two objects.   Then

$$f = \sqrt{\left(\frac{B.x.y}{y - x}\right)} \dots \quad \dots \quad \dots \quad (40).$$

Note; if in focussing the lens is moved, *B* must be ascer-
tained by measuring in each case the distance of the object
from some particular part of the moving lens or camera-
front, and deducting one dimension from the other.   If
on the other hand the screen is moved when focussing,

and the lens remains stationary, we need simply measure the distance between the two positions of the object.

(*f*) This method was especially devised by Mr. Dallmeyer for use with his focometer. Focus sharply on a near object, then move the object through a certain distance *l* farther from the lens, refocus and note the distance *c* through which the focussing-screen has been moved. Next, move the object through a distance again equal to *l* farther from the lens, refocus and note the movement of the focussing-screen from its last position, calling the distance *a*. Then

$$f = \frac{\sqrt{2l \times a \times c(a + c)}}{c - a} \qquad \dots \qquad \dots \qquad (41).$$

The lens must remain stationary during the different adjustments, hence this method is only applicable with a camera in which we move the screen to focus.

(*g*) This is a very excellent method, also devised by Mr. Dallmeyer. Reverse the lens in its flange on the camera, focus accurately on an infinite distance, and measure the distance from the ground glass to some definite point in the lens mount, say the lens hood. Call this distance *b*.

Remove the lens, replace it in its ordinary position, and find the infinity mark by focussing on a distant object. The screen is now at the back principal focus of the lens, while the other principal focus is at a distance *b* in front of the lens hood.

Next, focus on a near object at a distance *B* from the lens hood and measure the extension of the camera beyond the infinity mark (the extra-focal distance *x*). Deducting *b* from *B* we have the extra-focal distance of the object, and, therefore, from formula 7 (Sec 33)

$$f = \sqrt{(B - b)x} \qquad \dots \qquad \dots \qquad \dots \qquad (42).$$

(*h*) This method is advocated by Mr. Chapman Jones. Find infinity mark, then rack out and focus sharply on a near object of known size. Find the value of *R* by comparing size of image with that of object, and measure extension of camera beyond infinity mark to find *x*, then :—

$$f = \frac{x}{R} \qquad \dots \qquad \dots \qquad \dots \qquad (43).$$

This method is applicable with any form of camera. It is advantageous to use a divided scale as an object, and to measure the image with the same scale.

(*i*) This is a modification of the last method. Focus on a certain near object of known size, note the ratio of image to object (*R*) and mark position of focussing-screen. Repeat with object at a nearer distance and note new ratio *r*, and measure the additional extension of the camera, calling the extra distance *Z*. Then

$$f = \frac{Z}{R - r} \quad \dots \quad \dots \quad \dots \quad (44).$$

In this method we dispense with the infinity mark.

(*k*) Comparative methods.—Focus on an infinitely distant object, observe the size of the image, and then, with a pinhole in the place of the lens, produce an image of equal size from the same object. The distance from the pinhole to the screen is the focal length of the lens.

Or, if we have a second lens of known focal length, we can compare the size of the image produced by one lens with that produced by the other when each is focussed on the same infinitely distant object. The focal lengths are then proportional to the sizes of the images.

(*l*) Mr. Thomas Grubb's method is worked out geometrically.

At each side of the ground glass focussing-screen make a pencil mark, keeping the two marks a certain fixed distance apart, and equi-distant from the centre. Place the camera flat on a table covered with a sheet of white paper and focus on a very distant object, say a steeple or flag-staff, adjusting the camera so that the image exactly falls on one of the pencil marks. Then, using one side of the camera baseboard as a straight edge, rule a line on the paper to mark the direction of the camera. Next shift camera, altering its direction so as to bring the image over the other pencil mark (it is not necessary to rotate the camera about any particular centre) and again rule a pencil line on the paper, using the same ruling edge as before. This is all that need be done with the camera, which can now be removed. If necessary, produce the two converging lines on the paper until they meet in a point *A*, as shown in fig. 67. Bisect the angle *BAC* by the line

AD and draw *EDG* at right angles to *AD*, making *ED* equal to *DG* and the whole *EG* equal to the separation of the marks on the focussing-screen. Through *E* and *G* draw *EK* and *GH* parallel to *AD* and intersecting *BA* and *AC* in *K* and *H*. Join *KH*, cutting *AD* in *F*. The focal length is then equal to *AF*.

(*m*) A modification of the previous method. Grubb's method has the advantage of requiring very simple adjustments of the apparatus, and error is not likely to be introduced into the first part of the process if the object is sufficiently distant and the lens is free from distortion. The geometrical work is, however, very liable to error, and

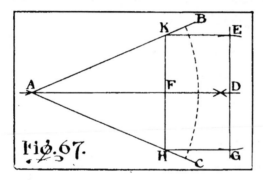

Fig. 67.

the length of *AF* may be better calculated if the angle *BAC* can be measured, for

$$AF = \tfrac{1}{2}EG \times cot.\tfrac{1}{2} \, BAC \quad \dots \quad \dots \quad \dots \quad (45).$$

The length of *EG* is known, and the angle *BAC* can be measured by a protractor, divided by two, and the cotangent of the result found from a table of natural tangents.

If the camera can be mounted on a pivoted arm that moves horizontally over an accurately divided quadrant circle, the angle *BAC* can be measured with great accuracy.

As regards the probable accuracy of the results obtained by any of these theoretically accurate methods, all require great care, while some are more liable to error than others.

Methods that involve the scale of the image are perhaps most liable to error, for it is a difficult matter to find the true ratio with extreme accuracy, and the presence (perhaps unsuspected) of a small amount of diaphragm distortion will upset the calculations. Other methods depend solely on accurate focussing and careful measurements, and a focussing eyepiece with clear glass screen is advisable, while an accurately divided measure is indispensable.

Grubb's method requires careful aiming of the camera and accurate draughtsmanship, and it should be noted that if the points K and H do not come exactly opposite one another so that the line joining them is precisely at right angles with AD there is an error somewhere in the drawing. It is just the kind of diagram that many draughtsmen will fail in, and very great care is necessary. The alternative method m has advantages if it can be carried out conveniently. With any of these methods it is advisable to make two or three determinations of focal length and average the results.

93. MEASURING EFFECTIVE APERTURE OF LENS.—In Sec. 9 it was pointed out that the effective aperture of a lens is represented by the diameter of the widest parallel incident pencil that can pass the lens, and this is not necessarily equal to either the diameter of the lens or of the diaphragm aperture, though it varies with the latter.

The simplest method of measuring effective aperture is to employ the lens as a collimator as described in Sec. 89. If we place a screen with a pinhole at the principal focus of the lens, and illuminate the pinhole by a powerful light behind, a parallel beam of light is projected by the lens. If this beam is received upon a screen the diameter of the circular disc of light thus produced is the diameter of the effective aperture. To ensure accuracy the screen should be close to the lens. A piece of ground glass may be placed in contact with the lens hood, or a piece of bromide paper may be inserted in the lens cap, and the disc be measured after development.

It is fairly evident that if a landscape lens with a front diaphragm is used, then the effective aperture is that of the diaphragm, but if a positive lens is in front of a diaphragm, as in a doubtlet or a reversed landscape lens, the effective aperture is greater than that of the diaphragm. If a negative lens is in front of the diaphragm the effective aperture is less than that of the diaphragm.

94. INCONSTANCY OF APERTURE.—From what has just been said it is clear that the effective aperture of a lens, and therefore its rapidity, may vary according to the direction of the incident light. Probably the only forms of lenses in which rapidity does not so vary are single lenses without a diaphragm, and perfectly corrected positive combinations with a diaphragm placed at the crossing-point.

In fig. 68 we illustrate a single lens with a diaphragm on the concave side, and therefore away from the crossing-point. The width of a pencil *ab* which comes to a focus

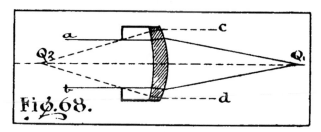

Fig. 68.

at Q_1 is equal to that of the diaphragm aperture, but the width of a pencil *cd* which comes to a focus at Q_2 is much greater; hence the lens is more rapid, or has greater intensity, if used with the diaphragm behind than it is with the diaphragm in front.

Q_1 is the image of a point at an infinite distance, and the pencil *cd* may be considered to be an emergent pencil forming an infinitely distant image of the point Q_2. Taking this point of view it appears that by bringing the object from an infinite distance to the point Q_2 we have increased the effective aperture from *ab* to *cd*, and, therefore, if the object had been left at an intermediate distance, the aperture would have been of an intermediate size. The extreme sizes can be easily measured, intermediate ones cannot without intricate calculations.

The formulæ for estimating exposure or depth are based on the assumption that ab is the constant aperture for an object at any distance. This not being always correct, the calculations are liable to error with near objects; exposure and depth both being overestimated, though possibly only to an inappreciable extent in the case of the former.

Under the Gauss theory we always represent the aperture as situated on the nodes and we measure it on the nodal planes, but make no allowance for variation. It would appear that the effective aperture must be constant if the diaphragm is situated at the crossing-point of a perfectly corrected lens. Inconstancy may be introduced by aberration, and must exist if the diaphragm is situated away from the crossing-point.

CHAPTER X.

95. SPECTACLE LENSES.—The term spectacle lens is applied to a simple single lens that by itself possesses every form of aberration, and with which the stop alone is relied upon as a means of correction. A meniscus lens (periscopic) concave side to the object is generally used, as it lends itself more readily to the production of a flat field, and the aberrations of the oblique pencils are not very violent as compared with direct pencils. On the other hand, longitudinal spherical aberration in direct pencils is considerable and has to be materially reduced by the stop, by which also coma is eliminated and the field flattened. At the best the angle of definition is narrow with any particular aperture. Positive chromatic aberration remains, while negative astigmatism, and inward or barrel distortion are introduced, and though effects of blur can be diminished by a small aperture these three aberrations cannot be corrected. In the case, however, of the positive chromatic aberration, as the visual yellow rays have a more distant focus than the actinic rays that are especially concerned in the formation of the image, the camera may be racked in slightly after focussing, to place the plate in the position of the actinic focus, for which purpose it is generally necessary to rack in for about $\frac{1}{50}$ the focal length of the lens.

Another method, due to Mr. Robert H. Bow, C.E., and adopted in the Busch "Vade Mecum" casket lens, is to use, when focussing, a positive supplementary lens that will reduce the visual focal length by one fiftieth part. After focussing this supplementary lens is removed, and the normal focal length is restored, leaving the screen at the actinic focus.

It should further be noted that when in ortho-chromatic photography a coloured-screen is used to cut out the more actinic rays, and a plate sensitive to yellow and red light is employed, the presence of chromatic aberration may be of little consequence.

By combining two single spectacle lenses to form a doublet, distortion can be corrected, and also coma. Astigmatism and chromatic aberration remain, but as the second lens may perform a little of the work that otherwise has to be done by the stop alone, a larger aperture can be used and a certain amount of rapidity can be gained.

Such a doublet is frequently styled a periscopic doublet, being formed of two single periscopic lenses. In this book, however, the term periscopic is applied to doublets in a different sense (see Sec. 15).*

96. LANDSCAPE, OR VIEW LENSES.—Generally speaking these titles are applied to single achromatic meniscus lenses, in which a cemented negative compensating lens is employed to secure achromatism and freedom from spherical aberration in small direct pencils. Other corrections depend on the stop, and hence, barrel distortion, astigmatism and secondary residual aberrations remain; the lens is slow and has a narrow angle of definition, and we may interpret the terms "landscape" or "view" to rather imply that the lens is not well adapted for any other purposes. In this case, however, it is not fair to apply the term to all single combinations, for it is possible by careful selection of glasses and curvatures to produce a single combination more or less free from aberration, and differing from a good doublet of similar power only in rapidity and covering angle.

It has before been pointed out that slight barrel distortion is advantageous rather than otherwise for purely landscape purposes, hence a lens producing this effect is at times very useful, though for many subjects it is not

* There is a particular lens called *the* "Periscope," which is a doublet combination of two single periscopic lenses. This was produced by Steinheil in 1865, and seems to have recently again come into use.

a serviceable lens. The presence of the other aberrations is of course just as detrimental in landscape subjects as in any others.

If we remove one of the combinations of a rectilinear doublet we can use the remaining combination and stop as a landscape lens, but, as a rule, it is inferior to the purposely made article, for the stop being too close to the lens, the aperture has to be greatly reduced to remedy curvature of the field. Much, however, depends on the importance of the part played by the stop in correcting the doublet, and if the single lenses are well corrected independently of the stop, either of them will make a good single lens.

Special rectilinear and wide-angled single landscape lenses are made, but these are not necessarily free from astigmatism ; on the other hand, an anastigmatic single lens is generally very nearly rectilinear, and will usually include a fairly wide angle.

97. RECTILINEAR LENSES.—By combining two single achromatic lenses to form a doublet diaphragm distortion can be corrected, but astigmatism remains with a slight residue of other aberrations. The increase in the number of lenses, however, gives opportunities of more perfectly compensating the aberrations, and hence a larger aperture can be used than with a single lens of the same focal length. Further, the stop may be closer to the lenses and so a wider angle of illumination can be included. In the best form of rectilinear doublet, astigmatism is practically the only form of aberration that is left, the mean astigmatic field being either flat or only slightly curved. If the lens is of wide-angle construction a small stop is necessary to flatten the field, and astigmatism becomes rather serious towards the margins of the plate.

It should be noted that, strictly speaking, the term rectilinear simply implies that the lens is free from distortion, and conveys no information with regard to other corrections. In a popular sense, however, the term is limited to doublets of the kind above described, though single landscapes may be, and anastigmats are usually also rectilinear.

10

A rectilinear (or, in fact, any other lens) may be styled "rapid" if it works well at an aperture not less than about $f11$.

98. ANASTIGMATIC LENSES.—Popularly this term is only given to lenses that are practically free from all the aberrations, but it may be applied to denote the special correction of astigmatism. Thus an anastigmatic lens may possess curvature of the field (see Sec. 55), and Ross' Concentric lens may be described as anastigmatic, it being free from astigmatism and curvature, though longitudinal spherical aberration is not compensated, and has to be reduced by the stop alone, which fact renders the lens slow.

The modern anastigmats (which are known by a variety of special titles) are distinguished mainly by the fact that spherical aberration is compensated at the same time that astigmatism is corrected, and the stop plays such a small part in the corrections that they can be made very rapid.

Anastigmatic doublets are of two classes, with separable and non-separable systems. In the former each system is perfect, and therefore the doublet may be divided into two single anastigmatic lenses, each of greater focal length than the doublet. The latter class are only perfect as a whole and cannot be divided.

99. PORTRAIT LENSES.—A portrait lens need not essentially be different from any other lens, but it is necessary that it should be very rapid for studio work, and that it should be corrected more especially for short distances. Some of the modern anastigmats appear to be equally well corrected for any distance, and to be well adapted for portraiture if rapid enough, but the term portrait lens is generally applied to lenses in which the corrections of oblique rays are to a large extent given up for the sake of extreme rapidity. It is not necessary that they should include a wide angle, in fact a very narrow angle of fine definition is all that is required, and this permits the use of a very large aperture, $f3$, or even larger. If used for purposes other than portraiture the aperture has to be reduced considerably, and then the portrait lens is likely to prove inferior to the more usual type of

doublet. The very large aperture and the nearness of the subject of course greatly reduces depth of field in portraiture. (See also Sec. 50.)

The great rapidity of portrait lenses renders them useful for some very high speed instantaneous work, but only a narrow angle of definition is included, and they are not suited for all subjects.

We are speaking here of only the ordinary type of rapid portrait lens. The term has also been applied to lenses that are well corrected for an aperture of $f6$, and that include moderate angles of definition.

100. ADJUSTABLE LENSES.—All the above types may be described as fixed lenses, but there are others that may be described as adjustable lenses.

One example of an adjustable lens is Dallmeyer's patent portrait lens, in which by slightly unscrewing one portion of the back combination a certain amount of spherical aberration can be introduced into direct pencils. As before explained, the portrait lens at a large aperture has a very small angle of definition and little depth. Extreme sharpness is therefore confined to the centre of the plate and to one plane of the object, and this effect is sometimes objectionable. The introduction of spherical aberration destroys this extreme local sharpness and renders the definition more uniform and the depth apparently, but not really, greater, (see pseudo-depth, Sec. 75).

Another adjustable lens is the Dallmeyer-Bergheim portrait lens. This is a narrow-angled doublet consisting of a front positive and a back negative lens, with a diaphragm in front of the positive lens. Each lens is a simple single uncorrected lens. To a certain extent the negative lens acts as a correcting or compensating lens, but there is a considerable amount of uncorrected spherical and chromatic aberration. This is left intentionally, as the purpose of the lens is to produce a soft image free from either objectionable blur or critical sharpness. The lens is adjustable inasmuch as the separation of the negative and positive lenses can be varied. This gives a considerable range of focal lengths in the one lens. For example, the No. 2 lens can be varied to give focal lengths of from 25 to 40 ins., and in this respect the Bergheim lens is similar to the telephoto lens, which is the most important form of adjustable lens.

101. TELEPHOTO LENS.—This consists essentially of a positive front, and negative back lens, with adjustable separation, differing from the Bergheim lens in that each system is, in itself, a completely corrected combination, usually of the doublet form. This ensures good definition under varying degrees of separation. The range of varying foci is also much greater than with the Bergheim lens. The peculiar advantage of the telephoto is one that is shared by all forms of periscopic doublets in which the front lens is positive and the back negative. The nodes of the lens are so far in advance of the front lens that a comparatively short extension of camera is required. If, for example, we compare the action of a rectilinear of 3 ft. focal length with that of a telephoto of the same power, formed of a 6-in. positive and 3-in. negative lens separated by $3\frac{1}{2}$ ins., the former requires an extension of the camera to at least 3 ft., the latter to only about 16 ins. Each would produce the same scale image, but the greater convenience of the telephoto lens is obvious.

Other peculiarities of the telephoto may similarly be illustrated by comparison. With the rectilinear the nodes would both be near the diaphragm slot and close together, and the front principal focus of the lens would therefore be about 3 ft. from the diaphragm slot; further, the lens might be of wide angle construction. With the telephoto lens (which is essentially a narrow angle lens) the node of emission would be $27\frac{1}{2}$ ins. in front of the positive lens, and the node of admission $24\frac{1}{2}$ ins. beyond the node of emission, while the front principal focus would be $36 + 24\frac{1}{2} + 27\frac{1}{2}$ ins. or 7 ft. 4 ins. in front of the positive lens. On account of this great distance of the front principal focus, we can only focus with the telephoto on an object that is apparently a considerable distance away, and the great nodal space of the telephoto greatly increases the distance between object and image.

Again; with the rectilinear we can only secure sharp focus on a given distance by altering the distance between the lens and the plate. With the telephoto we can focus in the same way, but there is an alternative method, for by altering the separation of the lenses we can alter the focal length of the lens to suit the position of the plate. It is recommended to focus first by varying the separation, and to make the final adjustment by the camera focussing arrangement. If we know the focal lengths of the positive and negative lenses, and their separation, the focal length of the whole combination and the positions of its nodes. can be determined by the equations given for combining lenses in Secs. 41 to 43.

The separation is, however, a difficult quantity to determine, and the focal length can be approximately arrived at as follows :—Secure sharp focus, then measure from diaphragm of front positive lens to focussing-screen, and multiply by the focal length of the positive lens divided by that of the negative. This multiplier is a constant for a particular lens ; thus in the example we have considered, it is equal to $\frac{6}{3} = 2$.

It is frequently convenient to compare the action of a telephoto lens as a whole, with that of its front positive lens used alone, and as the telephoto is commonly used upon objects at a great distance we may compare their actions when working only at their focal lengths. In the example considered we have a 6-in. positive front lens, and by placing a 3-in. negative lens $3\frac{1}{2}$ ins. behind, we have produced a telephoto lens of 36 ins. focal length, which acts precisely as a 36-in. ordinary lens would do. Therefore it is evident that the telephoto lens will form an image six times the linear dimensions of that produced by the 6-in. lens alone, and we may consider that the addition of the negative lens has magnified the image six times. Further, it is evident that this expansion of the image has reduced the intensity of its illumination in inverse proportion to its area. Thus, if the intensity with the 6-in. lens is $1/a^2$, it is $1/(6a)^2$, with the telephoto. The ratio aperture is therefore $1/6a$ with the telephoto if it is $1/a$ with the 6 in. ; and the fractional diameter of the aperture is $f/6a$ instead of f/a. Dividing the ratio aperture of the 6-in. positive lens by the magnification given by the negative lens, we obtain the ratio aperture of the telephoto lens. Thus the aperture of the 6-in. lens being $f8$, that of the telephoto is $f48$ if the magnification is six times.

The degree of magnification can be determined, without knowing the focal length of the telephoto lens, by the following exact rule given by Mr. Dallmeyer.

Having focussed, measure the distance of the negative back lens from the focussing-screen, divide by the focal length of the back lens, and add 1 to the result.

102. CASKET LENSES.—These generally consist of a set of single lenses of various powers with a mount into which they can be screwed to form either single landscape lenses or doublets of various focal lengths. The diaphragm (generally of the iris variety) forms part of the mount, and there is usually a little peculiarity in the manner in which the various apertures are marked. If they are marked with their fractional diameters it is obvious that these diameters are only correct when employing certain lenses of the set. Suppose a certain aperture to be marked $f16$, this can only apply to a certain combination, which we may assume to be of 8 ins. focal length. If we change the lenses to produce a focal length of say 10 ins., the aperture is no longer $f16$ but about $f20$. These variations being confusing and misleading it is generally best to mark the actual diameter of the diaphragm aperture, ignoring the effective aperture. Thus if the aperture is $\frac{1}{2}$ in. the effective aperture is approximately $f16$ for a lens of 8 ins. focal length and $f20$ for a 10-in. lens. Another method is to simply put a reference number to the aperture, and provide a table giving the approximate ratio aperture for lenses of various focal lengths.

Casket lenses differ greatly in their degrees of correction, and can be obtained with spectacle, achromatic, or anastigmatic single lenses. It can be readily seen that one particular combination of lenses is likely to be better corrected than the others, as the stop cannot be in the best possible position in all cases.

103. CONVERTIBLE LENSES.—To a certain degree any separable doublet is a convertible lens, but the term is more generally applied to lenses that are specially designed with a view to conversion. The Dallmeyer Stigmatic is a good example of the type, being a crossed doublet made up of two single combinations of different focal length. We can either use the doublet complete, or we can convert it

into single lenses of very fine quality, and thus there are three different focal lengths at our service.

Another example is one of the Cooke lenses. The ordinary Cooke lens is a non-separable triplet, but with the special type, one of the lenses of the triplet can be removed and replaced by a different lens, which alters the focal length of the whole combination without affecting its corrections.

104. NOMENCLATURE OF LENSES.—In many cases the titles given to lenses are self explanatory, but special names are sometimes used that do not clearly indicate the character of the lens.

The type of lenses described as "Rectilinear," in Sec. 97, includes also the lenses known as "Aplanats" and "Euryscopes"; the latter being usually of extra rapidity. Busch's "Pantoscope" is another lens of the same class, but made of lenses of very deep curvatures and including a very wide angle.

The "Anastigmatic" type, described in Sec. 98, includes not only the lenses known as "Anastigmats," but also the "Collinear," the "Stigmatic," the "Orthostigmat," the "Platystigmat," the "Cooke," the "Planar," the "Unar," and the "Protar," the last being also known as the "Satzanastigmat," or "Convertible Anastigmat." Among these the "Planar" is first and the "Unar" second as regards rapidity.

Ross' "Rapid" and "Universal Symmetrical" lenses belong to the class of rectilinears, and must not be confused with their "Universal Symmetrical Anastigmat." Their "Concentric" lens, before referred to, may be looked upon as a transitional type of lens. The "Antiplanet" is similarly a transitional lens between Steinheil's "Aplanat" and "Orthostigmat," being an attempt at producing an anastigmatic lens with the old varieties of glass.

By "Petzval" lenses we generally mean portrait lenses, made on the principles laid down by Petzval. Other Petzval lenses are practically out of date, but the portrait lens is still the standard type, though it has been modified and slightly improved by Dallmeyer and others.

APPENDIX.

(A).—COMPARATIVE FOCAL LENGTHS IN INCHES AND CENTIMETRES.

INS.	CMS.	INS.	CMS.	INS.	CMS.
·3937	1	9	22·86	19	48·26
1	2·54	9·054	23	19·685	50
1·575	4	9·449	24	20	50·8
2	5·08	9·842	25	21	53·34
2·362	6	10	25·4	21·653	55
2·756	7	10·236	26	22	55·88
3	7·62	10·63	27	22·44	57
3·149	8	11	27·94	23	58·42
3·543	9	11·022	28	23·622	60
3·937	10	11·416	29	24	60·96
4	10·16	11·811	30	25	63·5
4·33	11	12	30·48	25·590	65
4·724	12	12·204	31	26	66·04
5	12·7	12·598	32	27	68·58
5·118	13	13	33·02	27·559	70
5·512	14	13·386	34	28	71·12
5·905	15	13·779	35	29	73·66
6	15·24	14	35·56	29·527	75
6·299	16	14·567	37	30	76·2
6·693	17	15	38·1	31	78·74
7	17·78	15·748	40	31·496	80
7·086	18	16	40·64	32	81·28
7·48	19	16·533	42	33	83·82
7·874	20	17	43·18	33·464	85
8	20·32	17·716	45	34	86·36
8·266	21	18	45·72	35	88·9
8·661	22	18·504	47	35·433	90

This table can also be used for the purpose of comparing the sizes of English and Continental plates.

(B).—CORRESPONDING FOCAL POWERS AND FOCAL LENGTHS.

| FOCAL POWERS. | FOCAL LENGTHS. | |
DIOPTRIES.	CMS.	INS.
·25	400	157·48
·5	200	78·74
·75	133·3	52·49
1	100	39·37
1·25	80	31·49
1·5	66·6	26·24
1·75	57·14	22·49
2	50	19·68
2·25	44·4	17·49
2·5	40	15·74
2·75	36·36	14·31
3	33·3	13·12
3·5	28·57	11·24
4	25	9·84
4·5	22·2	8·74
5	20	7·87
5·5	18·18	7·15
6	16·6	6·56
7	14 28	5·62
8	12·5	4·92
9	11·1	4·37
10	10	3·93
11	9·09	3·57
12	8·3	3·28
13	7·69	3·02
14	7·14	2·81
15	6·6	2·62
20	5	1·96

(C).—SCALE TABLE OF CONJUGATE FOCAL DISTANCES FOR A LENS OF 1-IN. FOCAL LENGTH.

To use the following table find the required ratio in top horizontal and left vertical columns. The conjugate distances in inches for a lens of 1-in. focal length are then opposite the ratio numbers, the upper value being that of the shorter conjugate. The table includes ratios of from 1 : 25 to 25 : 1. Ratios between 1 : 10 and 10 : 1 are expressed in multiples; thus 1 : 4 is found under 3 : 12, and a scale of equal size by the ratio 10 : 10.

Example : to enlarge in the ratio of 4 to 3 (or 12 to 9); under 9 and opposite 12, we have 1·75 and 2·3 as the lesser and greater conjugates for lens of 1-in. focal length. The ratio of the conjugates being the same for any lens, we have only to multiply them by the focal length of the lens in use to find the actual focal distances. Thus, with a 6-in. lens they will be 7½ and 14 ins.

RATIO	1	2	3	4	5	6	7	8	9	10
10	1·1 11	1·2 6	1·3 4·3	1·4 3·5	1·5 3	1·6 2·6	1·7 2·428	1·8 2·25	1·9 2·1	2 2
11	1·09 12	1·18 6·5	1·27 4·6	1·36 3·75	1·45 3·2	1·54 2·83	1·63 2·571	1·72 2·375	1·81 2·2	1·9 2·1
12	1·083 13	1·16 7	1·25 5	1·3 4	1·416 3·4	— —	1·583 2·714	1·6 2·5	1·75 2·3	1·83 2·2
13	1·077 14	1·154 7·5	1·231 5·3	1·308 4·25	1·385 3·6	1·462 3·16	1·538 2·857	1·615 2·625	1·692 2·4	1·769 2·3
14	1·071 15	1·143 8	1·214 5·6	1·286 4·5	1·357 3·8	1·428 3·3	— —	1·571 2·75	1·642 2·5	1·714 2·4
15	1·06 16	1·13 8·5	— —	1·26 4·75	— —	-- --	1·46 3·143	1·53 2·875	— —	— —
16	1·062 17	1·125 9	1·187 6·3	— —	1·312 4·2	1·375 3·6	1·437 3·286	— —	1·562 2·7	1·625 2·6
17	1·058 18	1·117 9·5	1·176 6·6	1·235 5·25	1·294 4·4	1·352 3·83	1·41 3·428	1·47 3·125	1·529 2·8	1·588 2·7
18	1·05 19	1·1 10	— —	1·2 5·5	1·27 4·6	— —	1·38 3·571	1·4 3·25	— —	1·5 2·8
19	1·052 20	1·105 10·5	1·157 7·3	1·21 5·75	1·263 4·8	1·316 4·16	1·368 3·714	1·42 3·375	1·474 3·1	1·526 2·9
20	1·05 21	— —	1·15 7·6	— —	— —	— —	1·35 3·857	— —	1·45 3·2	— —
21	1·047 22	1·095 11·5	— —	1·19 6·25	1·238 5·2	— —	— —	1·38 3·625	— —	1·476 3·1
22	1·045 23	— —	1·136 8·3	— —	1·227 5·4	— —	1·318 4·143	— —	1·409 3·4	— —
23	1·043 24	1·086 12·5	1·130 8·6	1·173 6·75	1·217 5·6	1·260 4·83	1·304 4·286	1·347 3·875	1·391 3·5	1·43 3·3
24	1·041 25	— —	— —	— —	1·208 5·8	— —	1·291 4·428	— —	— —	— —
25	1·04 26	1·08 13·5	1·12 9·3	1·16 7·25	— —	1·24 5·16	1·28 4·571	1·32 4·125	1·36 3·7	— —

(D).—Relative Exposures for Different Scales of Image.

RATIO	1	2	3	4	5	6	7	8	9	·10
10 {	1·21 121	1·44 36	1·69 18·7	1·96 12·25	2·25 9	2·56 7·1	2·89 5·89	3·24 5·06	3·61 4·45	4 4
11 {	1·19 144	1·39 42·25	1·62 21·7	1·86 14·06	2·11 10·24	2·38 8	2·67 6·61	2·98 5·64	3·3 4·93	3·63 4·41
12 {	1·17 169	1·36 49	1·56 25	1·7 16	2 11·56	— —	2·5 7·36	2·7 6·25	3·06 5·4	3·36 4·84
13 {	1·16 196	1·33 56·25	1·51 28·4	1·71 18	1·91 12·9	2·13 10	2·36 8·16	2·6 6·8x	2·86 5·97	3·13 5·29
14 {	1·14 225	1·30 64	1·47 32	1·65 20·25	1·84 14·4	2·03 11·1	— —	2·46 7·56	2·69 6·52	2·93 5·76
15 {	1·13 256	1·28 72·25	— —	1·58 22·5	— —	— —	2·14 9·87	2·35 8·26	— —	— —
16 {	1·12 289	1·26 81	1·4 40	— —	1·72 17·6	1·89 13·4	2·06 10·7	— —	2·43 7·7	2·64 6·76
17 {	1·119 324	1·24 90·25	1·38 44·3	1·52 27·5	1·67 19·3	1·82 14·6	1·98 11·7	2·16 9·76	2·33 8·34	2·52 7·29
18 {	1·112 361	1·23 100	— —	1·49 30·2	1·63 21·1	— —	1·92 12·7	2·08 10·5	— —	2·41 7·84
19 {	1·106 400	1·22 110·25	1·33 53·7	1·46 33	1·59 23	1·73 17·3	1·87 13·7	2·01 11·3	2·17 9·67	2·32 8·41
20 {	1·102 441	— —	1·32 58·6	— —	— —	— —	1·82 14·8	— —	2·10 10·3	— —
21 {	1·096 484	1·19 132·25	— —	1·41 39	1·53 27	— —	— —	1·90 13·1	— —	2·17 9·61
22 {	1·092 529	— —	1·29 69·3	— —	1·5 29·1	— —	1·73 17·1	— —	1·97 11·8	— —
23 {	1·087 576	1·17 136·25	1·27 74·9	1·37 45·5	1·48 31·3	1·58 23·3	1·70 18·3	1·81 15	1·93 12·6	2·05 10·8
24 {	1·083 625	— —	— —	— —	1·45 33·6	— —	1·66 19·6	— —	— —	— —
25 {	1·081 676	1·16 182·25	1·25 87	1·34 52·5	— —	1·53 26·6	1·63 20·8	1·74 17	1·84 14·2	— —

This table gives relative exposures for the various scales provided for in table C. In each case the upper figure is the relative exposure for reduction, and the lower figure that for enlargement. As an example, suppose we know the required exposure for enlarging on a scale of 1 to 2 (or 5 to 10), and want the exposure for reducing on a scale of 5 to 3 (or 10 to 6); from the table the relative exposures are as 9 : 2·56; we must therefore divide our known exposure by 9, and multiply the result by 2·56.

(E, F, G, H).—Systems of Marking Apertures.

The rapidities of the different apertures included in these tables can be compared by the relative exposure numbers based on a unit exposure for f1 as given in the second column.

Classification by Exposure.

(E).—Uniform System.

APERTURE RATIO NO.	EXPOSURE NOS.		APERTURE RATIO NO.	EXPOSURE NOS.	
	UNIT f1.	U.S. UNIT f4.		UNIT f1.	U.S. UNIT f4.
1	1	1/16	11·312	128	8
1·414	2	1/8	16	256	16
2	4	1/4	22·624	576	32
2·828	8	1/2	32	1024	64
4	16	1	45·25	2304	128
5·656	32	2	64	4096	256
8	64	4	90·5	9216	512

This Table includes only the series of apertures recommended by the Royal Photographic Society.

(F).—Dallmeyer System.

APERTURE RATIO NO.	EXPOSURE NOS.		APERTURE RATIO NO.	EXPOSURE NOS.	
	UNIT $f1$.	DALLMEYER UNIT $f3\cdot16$.		UNIT $f1$.	DALLMEYER UNIT $f3\cdot16$.
1	1	·1	10	100	10
2·236	5	·5	12·25	150	15
2·74	7·5	·75	14·14	200	20
3·162	10	1	15·81	250	25
3·87	15	1·5	17·32	300	30
4·472	20	2	20	400	40
5	25	2·5	22·36	500	50
5·47	30	3	27·38	750	75
5·9	35	3·5	31·62	1000	100
6·32	40	4	38·73	1500	150
7·07	50	5	44·72	2000	200
7·42	55	5·5	50	2500	250
8·06	65	6·5	54·77	3000	300
8·66	75	7·5	63·24	4000	400

(G).—INTERNATIONAL CONGRESS (C.I.) SYSTEM.

SERIES	APERTURE RATIO NO.	EXPOSURE NOS. UNIT $f1$.	EXPOSURE NOS. C.I. UNIT $f10$.	SERIES	APERTURE RATIO NO.	EXPOSURE NOS. UNIT $f1$.	EXPOSURE NOS. C.I. UNIT $f10$.
	1	1	·01	b	21·88	480	4·8
b	1·935	3·75	·037	c	22·36	500	5
b	2·74	7·5	·075	d	24·49	600	6
a	3·535	12·5	·125	e	26·45	700	7
b	3·87	15	·15	a	28·28	8C0	8
a	5	25	·25		30	900	9
b	5·47	30	·3	b	30·96	960	9·6
c	5·59	31·25	·312	c	31·62	1000	10
d	6·12	37·5	·375	d	34·64	1200	12
e	6·612	43·75	·437	e	37·41	1400	14
a	7·07	50	·5	a	40	1600	16
b	7·74	60	·6	b	43·76	1920	19·2
c	7·9	62·5	·625	c	44·72	2000	20
d	8·66	75	·75	d	48·98	2400	24
e	9·35	87·5	·875	e	52·90	2800	28
a	10	100	1	a	56·56	3200	32
b	10·94	120	1·2	b	61·92	3840	38·4
c	11·18	125	1·25	c	63·24	4000	40
d	12·25	150	1·5	d	69·28	4800	48
e	13·225	175	1·75		70·71	5000	50
a	14·14	200	2	e	74·82	5600	56
b	15·48	240	2·4	a	80	6400	64
c	15·81	250	2·5	b	87·52	7680	76·8
d	17·32	300	3	c	89·44	8000	80
e	18·7	350	3·5	d	98	9600	96
a	20	400	4		100	10,000	100

Series of apertures that require exposure to be increased in the geometrical ratio of 2 are marked with corresponding letters. Series *a* includes the unit aperture of the C.I. system. Series *c* coincides very closely with the U.S. series given in table E, and is not very different from series *b*.

Classification by Intensity.

(H).—ZEISS SYSTEMS.

SERIES.	APER-TURE RATIO NO.	EXPO-SURE NO. UNIT $f1$.	INTENSITY NOS. OLD UNIT $f100$.	NEW UNIT $f50$.	SERIES.	APER-TURE RATIO NO.	EXPO-SURE NO. UNIT $f1$.	INTENSITY NOS. OLD UNIT $f100$.	NEW UNIT $f50$.
	1	1	10,000	2500	c	11·18	125	80	20
g	1·58	2·5	4000	1000	f	12·5	156	64	16
a	1·767	3·125	3200	800	g	12·65	160	62·5	15·625
c	1·975	3·9	2560	640	a	14·14	200	50	12·5
f	2·21	4·75	2048	512	c	15·81	250	40	10
g	2·236	5	2000	500	f	17 68	312	32	8
a	2·5	6·25	1600	400	g	17·88	320	31·25	7·81
c	2·795	7·8	1280	320	a	20	400	25	6·25
f	3·125	9·5	1024	256	c	22·36	500	20	5
g	3·16	10	1000	250	f	25	625	16	4
a	3·535	12·5	800	200	g	25·3	640	15·625	3·9
c	3·95	15·625	640	160	a	28·28	800	12·5	3·125
f	4·42	19	512	128	c	31·62	1000	10	2·5
g	4·472	20	500	125	f	35·36	1250	8	2
a	5	25	400	100	g	35·76	1280	7·8	1·93
c	5·59	31·25	320	80	a	40	1000	6·25	1·56
f	6·25	39	256	64	c	44·72	2000	5	1·25
g	6·32	40	250	62·5	f	50	2500	4	1
a	7·07	50	200	50	g	50·6	2560	3·9	·975
c	7·9	62·5	160	40	a	56·56	3200	3·125	·781
f	8·84	78	128	32	c	63·24	4000	2·5	·625
g	8·94	80	125	31·25	·f	70·72	5000	2	·5
a	10	100	100	25	f	100	10,000	1	·25

Series f includes the unit apertures of the Zeiss systems. Series a and c are the same as in last table.

(I).—Rules for Marking Apertures.

Classification by Exposure.

1. Square the ratio number to find relative exposure given in column headed " Unit f 1."
2. Divide relative exposure by 16 to find U.S. number.
3. Divide relative exposure by 10 to find Dallmeyer number.
4. Divide relative exposure by 100 to find C.I. number.
5. If desired to adopt any other unit aperture, the exposure number of any aperture can be found by dividing its relative exposure by the relative exposure for the unit aperture selected.

Classification by Intensity.

6. Multiply reciprocal of relative exposure by 10,000 to find Zeiss old system number, which is four times the value of the new system number.
7. The general rule for any other unit aperture is;—to find intensity number multiply the reciprocal of the relative exposure by the relative exposure for the unit aperture.

To find ratio number of an aperture marked by any of the above systems, reverse the processes described in above rules. For example, a U.S. number multiplied by 16 gives relative exposure for unit aperture of f 1, and the square root of the result is the ratio number. Or divide 10,000 by the Zeiss old system number to find the relative exposure for unit aperture f 1, and take square root of the result to find ratio number.

(J).—Table of Angles.

Find the diameter of the circle that is to be subtended by the angle, and divide by the focal distance of the lens from the plate. The quotient (T) is equal to twice the tangent of half the angle, but the value of the angle can be found very approximately from the following table.

IF T IS UNDER	THE ANGLE IS UNDER	IF T IS UNDER	THE ANGLE IS UNDER	IF T IS UNDER	THE ANGLE IS UNDER
Narrow Angles.		·95	51°	2·3	98°
·3	17°	1	53°	2·4	100½°
·35	20°	*Wide Angles.*		2·5	103°
·4	23°	1·1	58°	2·6	105°
·45	25½°	1·2	62°	2·7	107°
·5	28°	1·3	66°	2·8	110°
·55	31°	1·4	70°	2·9	111°
·6	33½°	1·5	74°	3	112½°
·65	36°	1·6	77°	3·2	116°
Mid Angles.		1·7	81°	3·4	119°
·7	39°	1·8	84°	3·6	122°
·75	41½°	1·9	87°	3·8	124½°
·8	44°	2	90°	4	127°
·85	46½°	2·1	93°	4·3	130°
·9	48½°	2·2	95½°	4·7	134°

To determine the covering angle the diameter of the circle is taken as equal to twice the distance from the principal axis of the lens to the farthest corner of the plate. To determine the view angle we take simply the diagonal of the plate as the diameter.

(K)—Diagonals of Stock Size Plates (Approximate).

PLATE.	DIAGONAL.	PLATE.	DIAGONAL.	PLATE.	DIAGONAL.
ins.	ins.	ins.	ins.	ins.	ins.
$2\frac{5}{16}$ × 1¾	2¾	6¾ × 3¼	7¼	12 × 10	15¼
2½ × 2	3¼	6½ × 4¾	7¾	15 × 12	19
3½ × 2½	4	7½ × 5	8¾	18 × 16	22
3¼ × 3¼	4¼	8½ × 6½	10¼	20 × 16	25¼
4¼ × 3¼	5	9 × 7	11¼	22 × 18	28¼
5 × 4	6¼	10 × 8	12½	24 × 20	31

(L).—Depth Constants in Inches and Feet.

FOCAL LENGTHS IN INCHES.

APERTURE RATIO NO.	1	3	4	4½	5	6	7	8	10
1	100 / 8·3	900 / 75	1600 / 133·3	2025 / 168·75	2500 / 208·3	3600 / 300	4900 / 408·3	6400 / 533·3	10,000 / 833·3
4	25 / 2·08	225 / 18·75	400 / 33·3	506·25 / 42·19	625 / 52·08	900 / 75	1225 / 102·08	1600 / 133·3	2500 / 208·3
5·65	17·68 / 1·47	159·15 / 13·26	282·9 / 23·58	358·08 / 29·84	442·08 / 36·84	636·6 / 53·05	866·48 / 72·2	1131·7 / 94·31	1768·3 / 147·36
8	12·5 / 1·04	112·5 / 9·37	200 / 16·6	253·12 / 21·09	312·5 / 26·04	450 / 37·5	612·5 / 51·04	800 / 66·6	1250 / 104·16
11·31	8·84 / ·73	79·57 / 6·63	141·46 / 11·79	179·04 / 14·92	221·04 / 18·42	318·3 / 26·52	433·24 / 36·10	565·87 / 47·15	884·17 / 73·68
16	6·25 / ·52	56·25 / 4·68	100 / 8·3	126·56 / 10·54	156·25 / 13·02	225 / 18·75	306·25 / 25·52	400 / 33·3	625 / 52·08
22·62	4·42 / ·36	39·78 / 3·31	70·73 / 5·89	89·52 / 7·46	110·52 / 9·21	159·15 / 13·26	216·62 / 18·05	282·93 / 23·57	442·08 / 36·84
32	3·12 / ·26	28·12 / 2·34	50 / 4·16	63·28 / 5·27	78·12 / 6·51	112·5 / 9·37	153·12 / 12·76	200 / 16·6	312·5 / 26·04
45·2	2·21 / ·18	19·89 / 1·65	35·36 / 2·94	44·76 / 3·73	55·26 / 4·6	79·57 / 6·63	108·31 / 9·02	141·46 / 11·78	221·04 / 18·42
64	1·56 / ·13	14·06 / 1·17	25 / 2·83	31·64 / 2·63	39·06 / 3·26	56·25 / 4·68	76·56 / 6·38	100 / 8·3	156·25 / 13·02

The constant is found under the focal length and opposite the aperture, the upper figure being the constant in inches, and the lower one the constant in feet. The constants for any other apertures can be found by dividing the constants for f1 by the ratio number of the aperture ; the constants for any other focal length by multiplying the constant for a focal length of 1-in. by the square of the focal length. Beyond giving the constants used in formulæ 21 to 26 this table serves other purposes. If we focus on infinity, the constant is the focal distance of the nearest object in focus. If we focus on an extra-focal distance equal to the constant, we obtain a maximum depth of field from approximately half the constant distance up to infinity. The constant is then the hyper-focal distance.

(M).—Consecutive Extra-focal Depths for Aperture f8 (Approximate).

FOCAL LENGTHS IN INCHES.									HYPER-FOCAL DISTANCES FOR
1	3	4	4½	5	6	7	8	10	
∝	∝	∝	∝	∝	∝	∝	∝	∝	
ft.	ft. in.	ft. in.	ft. in.	ft. in.	ft. in.	ft. in.	ft. in.	ft. in.	
1·0417	9 4½	16 9	21 0	26 0	37 6	51 0	66 8	104 0	f8
·5208	4 8½	8 4	10 6	13 0	18 9	25 6	33 4	52 0	f16
·3473	3 1½	5 7	7 0	8 8	12 6	17 0	22 3	34 9	f24
·2604	2 4	4 2	5 3	6 6	9 4	12 9	16 8	26 0	f32
·2084	1 11	3 4	4 3	5 2	7 6	10 3	13 4	20 10	f40
·1736	1 7	2 9½	3 6	4 4	6 3	8 6	11 2	17 4	f48
·1488	1 4	2 4½	3 0	3 9	5 4	7 3	9 6	14 11	f56
·1302	1 2	2 1	2 8	3 3	4 8	6 4	8 4	13 0	f64
·1157	—	—	2 11	4 2	5 8	7 4	11 7		f72
·1041	—	—	—	3 9	5 1	6 8	10 5		f80
·0947	—	—	—	—	4 8	6 0	9 6		f88
·0868	—	—	—	—	4 3	5 7	8 8		f96

These consecutive depths are very approximate, and are only applicable for aperture f8. Each vertical column is a complete series for one particular lens. Similar series for any other lens can be found by multiplying the figures in the first column by the square of the focal length. Taking any three consecutive distances in one vertical column, the lowest distance is the near, and the highest the far extra-focal depth of field when focussing on the middle distance. Every distance is also a hyper-focal distance for the aperture given in the last column.

(N).—APPROXIMATE INFINITY FOR LENSES OF VARIOUS FOCAL LENGTHS.

FOCAL LENGTH, INCHES.	DISTANCE OF FOCUSSING-SCREEN BEHIND PRINCIPAL FOCUS.			
	$\frac{1}{100}$ in.	$\frac{1}{250}$ in.	$\frac{1}{500}$ in.	$\frac{1}{1000}$ in.
1	3 yds.	7½ yds.	15 yds.	30 yds.
2	11 ,,	28 ,,	55 ,,	110 ,,
3	25 ,,	63 ,,	125 ,,	250 ,,
4	45 ,,	113 ,,	225 ,,	450 ,,
5	70 ,,	175 ,,	350 ,,	700 ,,
6	100 ,,	250 ,,	500 ,,	1000 ,,
7	136 ,,	340 ,,	680 ,,	1360 ,,
8	178 ,,	¼ mile	½ mile	1 mile
9¾	264 ,,	660 yds.	¾ ,,	1½ miles
11¼	351 ,,	½ mile	1 ,,	2 ,,
12½	434 ,,	1085 yds.	1¼ miles	2½ ,,
13¾	525 ,,	¾ mile	1½ ,,	3 ,,
16	700 ,,	1 ,,	2 ,,	4 ,,
17¾	875 ,,	1¼ miles	2½ ,,	5 ,,
19½	1056 ,,	1½ ,,	3 ,,	6 ,,
21	1225 ,,	1¾ ,,	3½ ,,	7 ,,
22½	1406 ,,	2 ,,	4 ,,	8 ,,
24	1600 ,,	2¼ ,,	4½ ,,	9 ,,
25	1 mile	2½ ,,	5 ,,	10 ,,
28	1¼ miles	3¼ ,,	6½ ,,	13 ,,
30	1½ ,,	3¾ ,,	7½ ,,	15 ,,
33	1¾ ,,	4½ ,,	9 ,,	18 ,,
35	2 ,,	5 ,,	10 ,,	20 ,,

By focussing accurately on distances not less than those given, we ensure that the focussing-screen is within $\frac{1}{100}$, $\frac{1}{250}$, $\frac{1}{500}$ or, $\frac{1}{1000}$ in. from the true principal focus.

INDEX.

(The Numbers refer to Sectional Paragraphs ; the Letters to the Appendix.)

PAGES ON WHICH SECTIONAL PARAGRAPHS COMMENCE.

Printed by Hazell, Watson, & Viney, Ld., London and Aylesbury.

CPSIA information can be obtained at www.ICGtesting.com
Printed in the USA
LVOW090819040212

266963LV00019B/211/A